Alistair Moffat

Alistair Moffat was born in 1950 in Kelso. After school he took degrees at St Andrew's, Edinburgh and London Universities. In 1976 he began a five-year period in charge of the Edinburgh Festival Fringe when it grew into the largest arts festival in the world. And then, for 18 years, he worked at Scottish Television, latterly as Director of Programmes and Chief Executive of Network Production. In 1999 he resigned these posts and came back to live in the Borders. His previous books include *The Sea Kingdoms: The Story of Celtic Britain and Ireland* and *The Borders*, both of which have been made into television series.

Other books by the author

THE EDINBURGH FRINGE
KELSAE: A HISTORY OF KELSO FROM EARLIEST TIMES
REMEMBERING CHARLES RENNIE MACKINTOSH
ARTHUR AND THE LOST KINGDOMS
THE SEA KINGDOMS
THE BORDERS: A HISTORY OF THE BORDERS FROM
EARLIEST TIMES

For Bina,
always with me

Contents

Acknowledgements

WRITING ANY STORY is always frustrating, the selection of ideas, episodes, words, clauses never quite right, sometimes even wildly, wince-makingly wrong. And the effect of those selections on the reader can produce all the wrong sort of reactions, clog perceptions with many misunderstandings, not be what I meant at all. Writing about my own life is even more frustrating. Only my eyes have seen it, nothing was reported to me except by my own senses and nothing lodged in my memory other than by way of my own impulses. And yet so much of what follows isn't quite right, not really what I meant at all. It was just the best I could do at the time. And in taking the foolhardy step of writing it down, I have risked a great deal. What follows is, after all, the story of parts of my life. If no-one likes it, or worse, everyone ignores it, then what does that say about me? 'That you've never had any common sense!' my Grannie Bina would have retorted immediately, perhaps even with an admonitory wave of her stick. OK Gran, I hear you. No common sense.

However I cannot settle for no acknowledgement of the role of other people in compiling this story. Everything in it is true, as true as I could remember it. But it may well not be everyone's truth. Real people, many of them still alive and well, populate these pages and I want to make it clear at the outset that I have not tried to speak for them (although sometimes I put words in their mouths), describe to them a world that they knew well or in any way attempt to act on their behalf. And if anyone takes offence, then all I can do is apologise in advance. It was never my intent to hurt.

In particular I want to thank my sisters, Barbara and Marjie, for all their love and forbearance. It's not their story either, but they were and remain closest to it.

I also want to thank warmly Caroline Knox and Hazel Wood at John Murrays for their unfailing patience and kindness to me and all their sustained efforts at making this a much better book than the manuscript they received a year ago. And to my agent, the redoubtable David Godwin, I owe a great debt for all his faith and persistence.

Prologue

MY MA WAS not a religious woman, but when she died in January 1990, my sisters and I still thought it right to ask Donald Gaddes, the Church of Scotland minister, to preside at the graveside and conduct a short service in her flat. Donald is a good man and he knew my Ma, but to remember her unbelief and to add something of our own to the formalities of the service my sisters asked me to write and read out a few words. It was a hard, hard thing to do properly and I'm glad to say that, despite one or two pauses, I got through it to the end. After the interment, the service and some tea with our family afterwards, I had a powerful urge to get outside and away. Having dealt with other people for two days, I wanted some time to be by myself.

I walked back down to the cemetery in the wintry sunshine to watch the gravediggers patch over the new grave with squares of turf. They nodded to me as they brushed the path and sorted the wreaths and flowers into a neat rectangle. A long time ago I played rugby with one of them. 'You all right?' he asked. 'Aye, fine. Fine thanks.' He smiled and pushed his barrow towards the sheds and the yard at the far end of the cemetery.

I had no anger or any sense of guilt at my Ma's death. Just an immense sadness that she was no longer in the world. I loved her and I think I did all that I could for her, and certainly all that she wanted me to do. By the end of her life, she had had enough of it and wanted to die. Her health was failing, which she hated, and at seventy-four, a welcome heart attack took her where she wanted to go, to where my Dad was waiting for her.

I still think about her most days. I know that her love was not a mortal bond and it will never fail me. But she was part of an older Scotland, disappearing fast like leaves in the winter winds, and aside from her grandchildren, she had really lost interest in tomorrow. My sisters and I had moved away. And I think she knew that if distance and diffidence had gone on a long time it would have coloured her feelings for everything, including her precious family, and that we would have been left with a dominant memory of a silent, expressionless, incontinent geriatric. It was right that she died while she could still light a room with her smile.

I looked down at her flowers and picked up all of the cards and put them in my pocket. We could all look at them later, maybe much later. Just as I made to turn away, the inscription on the grey, polished granite headstone caught me. I hadn't wanted it to, I was burying my Mother today. It read 'John Lauder Moffat 1916–1986', and that was it. No details, definitely no details, just my Dad's name and the dates and a full stop chiselled at the end. 'That's all he would have wanted,' said someone. Perhaps, but it was a great deal less than I or my sisters needed. Looking at the three names and two dates, it came in on me how little we understood about him. I knew he wasn't there, nobody is there in cemeteries except a lot of living people wandering about wondering how they should be feeling. And no point in standing in front of a gravestone and trying to extract some meaning from a piece of cold granite. The problem was that he wasn't anywhere to be found. Not anywhere. Unlike with my Ma, I had come to no peaceful accommodation with my Dad's death, even though it had been five years since.

I found myself thinking more and more about my childhood, how it happened around my Ma and my Dad, and especially around my Grandmother, Bina. It seemed to me that I could accept my Ma's death because I felt I knew her and I understood where she came from. Her sisters, her nieces and nephews and grandchildren had all come to the funeral that day. We knew them, cared about them as family, visited their houses in Hawick and elsewhere in the Scottish Borders, went to weddings, christenings and funerals. When Bina died, she just disappeared out of my life, leaving me nothing but a vacuum. I was abroad at the time and had no idea that she had gone and left me. And when my Dad died, there were no relatives except us, absolutely none at all. All the cords to his coffin were taken by his children and his friends. It was as though he had no family behind him. All we knew was Bina, the woman he called 'Ma' and who lived with us all our young lives. When I was a child he refused all questions about the past and persistence could be met with a smack, or later, even a punch. A long time ago I learned to stop asking.

Walking back up the brae to my Ma's flat in the January of 1991, I resolved that one day I would take some time and try to find out who Bina really was, where her family came from, who my Dad was, and what made him the man I remember. With my Ma's death, they had all gone, those people who raised me, made me whatever I had become. Somehow I felt I could begin to ask the unanswered questions about my childhood without risking rage, shame or upset, or untruth. And more than that, I wanted to think about my childhood before it became the burnished jewel of selective memory, each anecdote embellished by repetition, enhanced by comparison with a dull geriatric present, youth as it is too often remembered by the old – impossibly gilded, bent out of shape by the need to console.

Early in the summer of 1999 I put aside my work and decided to drive down to Kelso to visit the cemetery and put some flowers at my parents' headstone. I couldn't do the same at my Grannie Bina's for the good reason that she doesn't have one. My Dad always claimed that he couldn't afford a stone for his Ma, but it seemed more likely to me that it was the detail that daunted

PART I

stakes laced together with twisted wire top and bottom was unrolled from its bundles and stitched to rows of posts, the garden ground roughly levelled and the new occupants left to get on with it.

Which they did with gusto. The intensive domestic cultivation of the Second World War ingrained gardening disciplines which quickly converted the virgin plots into rowed, hoed and watered cornucopia. Out of an area no bigger than 30 by 10 yards produce flowed, from midsummer lettuce up to Christmas Brussels sprouts and potatoes left in the ground under withered yellow shaws and happed with straw. When the nearby rugby ground was scoured flat, some of the topsoil was dumped on the gardens of Inchmead Drive and it allowed even the most amateurish horticulture to burgeon. At No. 42 my Dad laid out three plots divided by transverse paths which were in turn connected by a wider path running down one side of the garden. He allocated the plots to tatties, tatties and other things. What turned out to be a dank and dark shed was built at the southern foot of the garden, and later, a greenhouse beside it for tomatoes. My Dad kept back seed potatoes from each year's harvest and laid them out in wooden trays in the shed where after a while sickly-looking white shoots curled out of them. Once I broke them all off and brought them into the kitchen to show Gran. When Dad came home with packets of seeds from Laing and Mather's, he sprinkled their contents like magic dust in shallow trenches made with the blunt edge of a rake. Once the magic dust had been covered over and watered, Dad speared each packet with a short stick and stuck it in at the end of the row. Our lettuces never looked anything like the lush green illustrations, and by the time they poked though the soil spring rain had washed the packets white. The northern limits of the World were marked emphatically by the side of the house where a rickety (it was always rickety) green trellis went up around an arch with a gate in it.

Such were the edges of the geography of the World. Fences were fences and neighbours on all sides respected them, and more important, other children entered only by invitation, and certainly never in anger or pursuit. I could run faster than Terror Scott, and after I gained the sanctuary of the trellis gate, he skidded to an impotent halt. So secure were the boundaries of the World that I could even turn and dare to glare at the seething Terror for a while, and when that grew stale, I improvised a few hand and finger gestures. When fighting on the pavement of Inchmead Drive with big Ali Boompa, some of his supporters and his dog, was not going well, desperate measures were being frantically assessed. No. 42 was too far but the front gate of 44 might be gained with a sprint. Despite Boompa's close pursuit I made it, ran down the side of 44, turned and kicked him in the shin before vaulting the picket fence back into the World. Suddenly my enraged opponent seemed isolated, hopping on one leg in someone else's garden, and without another hostile move, he fled.

Boompa was not intimidated by our neighbours. Auntie Grey and Bob were mild-mannered, somewhat cultured pensioners. It was convention that suddenly overwhelmed him, the fact that he found himself uninvited, even unknown, in someone else's garden. I doubt if the incident even registered with Auntie Grey. She was a dainty woman who wore her hair up, held with combs and pins, and whose house had carpets, little tables beside the chairs with magazines on them and polished brass things in the fireplace. I never once went into the living room and saw all of these things only when Auntie Grey opened the door. Their wireless seemed to be on all the time and the low murmur of a perpetual conversation punctuated by snatches of jaunty music floated across the picket fence. Bob did drawings. Mostly still lives, they were bewilderingly beautiful studies of difficult objects like glass bottles or cockerels. When he gave me one to hold in my grubby hands I must have examined it in the same way as African Bushmen first beheld photographs – in slack-mouthed, wide-eyed astonishment. How could a normal person in Inchmead Drive, Kelso, Roxburghshire, Scotland, Great

Britain, Europe, The World, The Solar System, The Universe do this? The delicate shading, intricate cross-hatching, perfect circles and straight lines probably made me turn over the drawings to see if they really were two-dimensional.

While Uncle Bob tried to interest me in art, Auntie Grey introduced me to mystery. The day Baby Helen came the World changed. I didn't remember her as a baby for the good reason that I had been one too at the time, but when she later reappeared in the World in a frock, we held hands. All the time. Exquisitely beautiful with shining blond hair and enough teeth for a smile, she made me stare, and hold her hand. I have no photograph of Baby Helen, only a crystal memory, and no wish to discover whatever became of her. When Auntie Grey died and Bob moved away, Baby Helen never came back to see me again. Not ever.

Across the fence at the bottom of the garden Mr Smeaton growled and prowled. A small man, he was a monumental sculptor with a workshop handily placed near the Parish Kirk cemetery and only a stone's throw from the new one beyond Shedden Park. 'Wharrayelookinat!?!' I was only looking through the blackcurrant bushes, watching him forking horse muck into his tattie patch. 'I see you!' But I'm not doing anything bad. 'Come out! Come out!' No, I'm not. 'I won't bite.' Yes you will. Mr Smeaton stood up from his digging, rearranged his orange tweed bunnet back into exactly the same place (the shock of once seeing him without it was profound, it seemed to diminish him, make his head shrink, not be him), and smiled a headshaking smile before bending to his work again.

Did he dig the graves as well? Put the dead people in the coffins and nail down the lids on them? And then put a big stone on top of them so they couldn't get out in the event of a tragic mistake having been made at the hospital before he started with his chisels and mallet. Perhaps they could hear him clinking away above them with his tools on the headstone? Cackling. 'Come out. Come out, if you can. Heh, heh, heh.' Had he already made a special one for himself and Mrs Smeaton, and put it in the garden shed so it would be handy, just leaving one date to be done by his apprentices? And how did Mr Smeaton decide about the trapdoor? Or did God tell him beforehand that a new coffin was to be for a good person and that he should leave the lid loose, maybe just stuck on with Sellotape, so that they could get out and float up to Heaven to be with the angels and their harps on God's Right Hand when nobody was looking, or they all had their eyes shut praying? But if it was for a bad person who had done a lot of swearing, even under their breath, did he put a trap-door in the bottom of the coffin so that when the big hole was dug for them they would drop straight down, down and down, all the way down a long black tunnel and fall right into the flames of the Fires of Hell?

'Hey!' Mr Smeaton straightened up from his digging (you'd think he did enough digging at his work). 'What's that behind you!' I thrashed out of the bushes, snapping stalks and trampling blackberries, and raced for the sanctuary of the back door and Bina's kitchen.

On the other side of the World, across the fence by the garden path, lived Sybil Withers and the Pipe Major. Because 42 was the end house in a terrace of five, we had direct access to the garden around the gable end and through the trellis. If Sybil and the Pipe Major had something large or mucky to deposit in their garden, they had to carry it for miles, a long way around the other end of the terrace, through an arch next to the Harveys' house, down a path past Mrs Middlemas' and along another path past the foot of the Dummas' garden, and Malcolm Thomson's until, much later, they came to the bottom of their own garden. Which they did often. So powerful were the conventions of the fences that not only could their magic repel Terror Scott and Ali Boompa, but they also deterred big men like the Pipe Major. Mrs Withers was also tall (but didn't march and swing her arms), so tall that she once picked me up and laid me out on the settee in the living room at 42. I had fallen out of our car, knocked myself out on the tarmac and for reasons lost in the confusion of an emergency, my Dad, who was driving, did not carry me into the house. Perhaps he didn't notice I had fallen out. And it was against the confusing floral-print bosom of Mrs Withers that I came round and re-entered the World.

After the accident and the affront of Mrs Withers doing the needful for her only grandson, my Gran kept a much closer eye on me. My Ma was out at her work, my older sister at the school and Marjie still in the pram, clipped in place by reins after I had tipped her out in Shedden Park. That left my Gran as sole custodian, a large sixty-three-year-old woman exasperated by a skittering, skinny little kid.

'Here! Come here where I can see you!' she roared up the summer garden, banging her stick on the side of the coal box. I was hiding in the tattie shaws from Japanese patrols, lying absolutely still on the damp black earth between the dreels.

'Now come you here to me!' Her voice was far away from the luminous emerald green jungle of stalks and shoots. I could tell my Gran was still sitting down, the *People's Friend* beside her on the bench by the back door. After a few seconds she tutted and grunted, using her stick to push herself up on to her feet: a big, stout, stooping woman who always wore slippers and rocked from side to side when she walked. Getting up was a business for Gran, particularly on a hot, drowsy afternoon. If I made her walk up the stony path in her soft slippers and on her corns, the least I'd get would be a cuff round the ear.

'Ta Daa!' I stood up out of the shaws. The old woman blew out her cheeks, shook her head and sank back down gratefully.

'As sure as a cat's a beast, you'll have me in Melrose.' It was not the town that worried Bina but the presence of a large and forbidding mental hospital on its outskirts. Dingleton served the Tweed Valley and was the ultimate destination for those Borderers bothered with their nerves.

Gran rarely went beyond the Near World that lay just outside the back door. Perhaps the uneven walking was too difficult. To please her and let her doze over the *People's Friend*, I played there most of the time, running Dinky cars along the concrete where it was smooth and building US Cavalry forts where the gravel allowed construction. A few bedraggled flowers had been shoved into the border of the tattie plot nearest the house and they supplied enough cover for Japanese soldiers to ambush a convoy of Dinkys and clockwork trains on their way to relieve Fort Apache, which had recently been captured by Dan Dare, Digby and Biggles, in a surprise aerial assault. Damp earth could easily be flattened into winding roads and crumbly tunnels made through the banked up tattie shaws ('Wait till your father sees that when he gets home!').

Once, a careering Dinky, completely out of control, flew past the petrol station outside the gates of Fort Apache and disappeared under the coal box. They probably heard me in Melrose. It was my green Vanwall racing car, and Jack Brabham was driving. In the end, hours later, my Dad got it with a hoe and a torch after he came back from his work.

'Christ almighty! Stop your noise. Here's the bloody thing!'

'He wouldn't eat his dinner,' said my Gran in an oblique attempt at an excuse, 'and there's doughboys for tea.'

Grub. Food. 'Here comes the lorry, down the red hill.' 'It's on the table. Now!' 'It's getting cold.' 'Get that knocked into you!' My Gran coaxed me with stories designed to distract sufficiently so that I would eat without thinking, because when I was little I wouldn't. All sorts of stratagems and threats were used and the achievement of a clean plate received such affirmation that I still look up for applause after supper. Much later my Ma confessed that when I was born I was so ugly that she rejected me. Completely. Could not bear to have me in the same room. I looked like Winston Churchill in bad fettle. And because she had septic breasts, it was impossible for her to feed me. I'm told that my Gran made up bottles of 'Formula' which I guzzled through a rubber teat. Already a large baby, I grew fast in every direction, intent on thriving, oblivious to the emotional agonies, jealousies and rivalries swirling around my cot.

But when I could close my mouth and keep it pursed shut, I began to refuse food, and to my Mother's guilty horror I grew slowly upwards but not outwards. Neither cash nor tradition was available to my Gran when she took on the role of cook and force-feeder. No fridge existed to store food and therefore very little choice was possible, and in any case a lifetime of making ends meet had allowed my Gran only a narrow range of recipes, all of which she knew by heart, measuring quantities by a handful and a pinch. And so my reluctant appetite could not be tempted by a variety of impossible fancies, but only an everyday sort of menu supplemented by threats and cajolement.

Even though I rarely consented to eat what she made, I can remember sitting 'where I can see you' in the kitchenette, watching my Gran cook. She blethered all the time, sometimes to me, sometimes to the cooker, sometimes to the ingredients, often to 'My God in Heaven!' Her staple was broth, what she called kail and always refered to in the plural. 'They're best on the second day.' It was a thick soup made in as big a pan as could fit on the electric ring. Kail lasted for many days, often diluted with water and more ingredients added. Everything was boiled: cabbage, tatties, onions, carrots, a mixture of grains and red lentils called 'Tipitin', and what my sisters and I came to call 'sloshy meat'. This was usually the cheapest cut of beef with plenty of fat on it and sometimes skin. No sense of what might be healthy or unhealthy existed in my Gran's cooking. Calories were what mattered, filling your stomach until it was impossible to eat any more. Everything that was edible was good for you, because it was edible. Kail was taken with slices of plain bread and Stork margarine (butter cost more and went off quickly, even on the stone shelf in the larder) at dinnertime and the meat lifted out and eaten with tatties at teatime. My Ma or Gran also always made supper at about 8 p.m. and the fourth meal of the day was generally sandwiches. And if they had potted meat in them, I wouldn't eat them either.

I still won't willingly have soup and in 1953 my Gran was forced to improvise her way around that profound dislike. For my Dad's tea she often made stew with dumplings called 'dough-boys' (I later discovered that this was the name given to American soldiers in the First World War), and if it was to last over two days, I got for my dinner some reheated with tatties mashed with the top of the milk. I liked the tatties well enough. A boiled egg chopped up with salad cream was sometimes tried, as well as common items like mince and tatties (I refused to eat it if there were carrots chopped in). Anything I left, and that was likely most of it, was immediately eaten by my Gran. The waste of food was not so much abhorrent to her as inconceivable.

The annual gala performance was elderberry wine. Before they attracted the label 'wild food' all sorts of harvests were routinely gathered from the fields and woods around towns like Kelso. Mushrooms from old pasture, raspberries and brambles from hedges and woodland, fish legally and illegally taken from burns and rivers, and rosehips gathered from prickly bushes to be sold at ninepence a pound for making Delrosa which was spooned into sickly, skinny children from Glasgow. But elderberries were the most colourful and dramatic crop. They grew everywhere and with purple fingers and faces children brought back bucketfuls on autumn days. Using the giant enamelled jam pan my Gran tipped in the berries, stalks and all, to boil with sugar for the best part of a day. After it had cooled she made toast, almost black and brick-hard. She slathered one side of each slice liberally with yeast and floated it on top of the purple-black wine so that infusion was gradual, and mysterious. After sieving it through muslin, and with a ladle and funnel, she filled old lemonade bottles with the fermented result and screwed the black cork stoppers in tight before setting the batch on the cold shelf in the larder. Sometimes not tight enough. 'What in the name of God!?!' Mostly the explosions forced out the cork and only a little of the dark wine, but my Dad must have imagined himself back at El Alamein. It was nectar, rich and aromatic like port wine. And Barbara, Marjie and I got some when we were ill. Which was often.

Liz Gladstone knew what was good for you, and her sister, Peg Murray, knew too. Once when I wasn't well she terrified the illness out of me with soap and water, and some rough handling. Gripping me under the oxters and pulling me into her pillowy bosom, Liz lifted me up on to the draining board next to the kitchen sink.

'Now.' She peered into my widening eyes. 'Let's just see what's what.'

Peg nodded, Bina watched over her shoulder and Liz showed she meant business by taking off her black beret.

'Stick your tongue out.'

Certainly.

'Cheeky little bugger. Stick your tongue out and open your mouth at the same time.' Liz's steady, wheezy breathing was so close I felt as though she was doing it for me.

'No. Nuh. Nothing. Nothing at all.' She glared at me through narrowing eyes and took hold of my head, rotating it through impossible angles. 'But now that you're up here, you'll be none the worse for a good wash.'

And with a facecloth like sandpaper, hot water straight out the tap and a square bar of green Fairy soap, Liz set about scrubbing out of me whatever it was she had failed to diagnose.

'That's better now!' Was it buggery.

What delivered my early upbringing into the arthritic hands of my Gran and her friends was economics. She was at home all day, was a good cook, could manage some housework (particularly sewing and mending) and above all saw childminding as a natural role, leaving my Ma free to go out and earn some welcome extra cash. Much later I understood that she was in fact saving to buy a house, something rare amongst working people in the Fifties. But when a beautiful old riverside property in Kelso, known as The Dispensary, came on the market at £400, my Dad shook his head. 'A millstone round our neck.' And to make matters worse, he told one of his friends about it, and he went and bought it. Decades later my Ma still wept over The Dispensary.

Beyond the Jap-infested tattie shaws lay the Far World, the bottom of the garden, an exposed outpost flanked on three sides by unexplored, forbidden territory. Auntie Grey's gooseberry bushes offered enough dense cover to reach the rhubarb buckets completely unseen by enemy patrols. But when the fat, yellowing, veined goosegogs were ripe the sniper might be delayed, the mission sometimes abandoned. Like coconuts or pomegranates (or maybe even melons?), rhubarb was jungle food, the sort of thing foraging commandos just had to make do with on patrol. Lifting the tin buckets off the dark and secret world of livid red stalks and emerald green leaves was a miniature adventure. The rhubarb never seemed the same twice, seemed to grow magically, unnaturally. Having broken off an eye-wateringly sour stem, I held my breath, listened for a tell-tale twig snapping, and if none did and the coast was clear, quickly crossed the path to take cover in the greenhouse. My Dad had built a wooden frame out of railway sleepers and they made up enough of the walls to crouch behind them out of sight and force down a bite of the sharp stalk.

It was always breathless and stifling in amongst the bitter-green smell of the tomatoes and musty compost, but this was the jungle, the place where the Evil Empire of Nippon would be stopped. In the heavy, hushed quiet you could easily hear the deadly buzz of mosquitoes, the ear-piercing squawk of parrots and the faintest trill of 'Colonel Bogey' being whistled away in the distance.

Once my Gran let the budgie out in the greenhouse. Joey used to be allowed to flutter around the living room, but, using his needle-sharp claws, he could perch far out of reach on the embossed wallpaper or on the pelmet above the window. 'Here, here. Tweet, tweet. Here, here. Little bugger.' Gran swore at him and waved the handle of her mop at the budgie, but there was no chance of catching him before he had shat all over the new settee. The greenhouse seemed like a good alternative, except that there was only a glass door between Joey and the wide, wide world. Where there were cats, and probably not enough budgies on the run to make a flock.

For what must have been a long time Gran and I crouched and sweated and swore in the greenhouse, and Joey flapped unenthusiastically between the furry stems of the tomatoes, and shat harmlessly on the compost, and Gran. With some crumbled millet we got him back into captivity and the cage was rehung on its stand in the living room. Joey died during an episode of *Sergeant Bilko* in 1959. I wept and Gran suggested we get a cat.

The Far World was bordered entirely by the gardens of gardeners, and no other children. Such was the strength of the convention of fences that short-cuts were only considered in dire emergencies, mercy dashes to the lav or escape from the Woodhead gang. If I wanted to play with Colin Purves and his guinea-pig, Little Colin, or with Bindie McCombie, Bob Thomson or Cobey, a journey beyond the trellis was involved. And that needed Gran to agree, and that involved answering questions. 'Nothing.' 'Dunno where.' 'Maybe.' Gran could roar across a dozen gardens and see through walls when any of her exhaustive list of prohibitions were threatened.

However, there were regular and permissible rendezvous which got around my Gran's ban on free association amongst the under fives. Baker's vans, butcher's vans, grocery vans and many others now seem all to have disappeared from small-town Scotland's streets but in the early 1950s they arrived every day. Jock Trummle could pull out floury wooden trays of cakes, breads, teabreads, scones, fancies, tattie scones, summertime strawberry tarts, and best of all, hazel cakes. Pan, plain, well-fired, bran, brown and fancy breads were all baked at Jack Scott's, Hossack's and Pie Ried's by the ghostly men who flitted past 42 at 4 a.m. every morning but one. And every morning but one their produce came fresh down Inchmead Drive. Johnstone

Scott called my Gran 'Bina' and passed on the gleanings of gossip gathered on his round with the Store butcher's van. It had 'Fleshing Department' painted on the side. Fish came on Fridays from Eyemouth, and Ingan Johnnies from France with their plaits of onions strung over the handlebars of antique black bikes. It was a long way to go back to load up every morning.

Each week in the winter people from Africa came to Inchmead Drive in a coal lorry. When they blinked or smiled enough to show their teeth, their black faces only seemed blacker. Once the coal lorry had stopped and they had shouted their arrival in the street, Bina went out to read the chalked prices on the blackboard attached to the back of the cab. 'Shilbottle 7/6d the hundredweight, Scremerston 6/8d, Dross 5/-.' The Africans wore body armour, like the Romans, except black, so that when they backed into the side of the lorry and put their hands over their huge shoulders to grab the top corners of a coalbag, the sharp edges of the lumps didn't scratch them. I didn't believe Bina when she explained. One of them chased me with his black hands once, all the way round to the back door. And that proved it, about the Africans, whatever it was.

When Ethel and Doddie came with the logs, they just stopped the horse and cart, didn't shout, took the money, put the logs round the back, wore no armour and never chased anybody. In fact they always seemed a bit lost themselves, never speaking to anyone, or each other, except when Ethel gave Doddie a doing about something or other. And Wilson Simpson, the chimney-sweep with two surnames, was always too busy shouting up the chimney and blethering to Bina to bother me or anybody else. His springtime arrival ('Never cast a clout till May is out.' What? Just another daft thing adults said to each other) began with the ritual of the papers. Saved up from firelighting for a week, the *Scotsman* was laid like crazy paving from the front door through the front lobby, under the dead fox's head over the door, into the living room and across to the fireplace. Wilson Simpson, or Simpson Wilson, his wee brother, brought in a giant hoover big enough to suck up small animals, and then lots of sooty blankets which he used to cover up the fireplace and wedge the sucking bit into the bottom of the grate. Once he had done that Bina and I followed him outside to watch him tell the apprentice on the roof to start shoving down the brushes. Then we all nipped back in to watch Wilson switch on the giant hoover and make sure that Joey's feathers weren't fluttering as it sucked up all the falling soot. Wilson and his apprentice were allowed to drink their tea and eat Bina's shortbread with black hands. And she never said a thing to them. Never.

Show business announced itself to Inchmead Drive with the tinkle of Forte's ice-cream van at the weekends and the summer evenings, and as a reward for not swearing on a Sunday Gran used to buy me a vanilla cone with Technicolor raspberry sauce squirted over it. On hot days we ate melting cones from the bottom up before clamping our mouths over the top and forcing the ice-cream downwards with our tongues so that none could escape. The shocked hush at Bob Thomson dropping his cone was quickly replaced by admiration when he went down on all fours like Mrs Hall's cat to lick up what actually wasn't touching the tarmac.

One blazing Sunday morning in July Dominic Forte rang the doorbell. I thought he was just early and looked about his person for a cone or a scoop before I began to listen to what he was saying. Dominic was excited.

'Where your father? Where Jackie? I need Jackie quick, quick.'

Of all days, on a Bank Holiday July weekend when Forte's would sell many gallons of their own ice-cream, the machine needed to whip and agitate the wonderful mixture had broken down. Dominic, my Dad and I rushed down the street to the café. Years later Dad explained that the motor had burnt out on what looked to me like a spin-drier. He could sort that but a much more serious problem was that the steel paddle which essentially made the ice-cream had cracked and threatened to shear off. Dominic was distraught, and my Dad shoved his bunnet back on his head and blew out his cheeks.

'Go back up the street and see what Tom Melrose is doing.'

Tom was an engineer, a highly skilled lathe-worker to trade, and he lived opposite us in Inchmead Drive. After a breathless report back that he was just finishing his breakfast, we drove up in the ice-cream van (disappointingly, no tinkles, but I waved at a few baffled people) and collected Tom who opened up the workshop.

'We'll just have to make a new bit.'

With one leg shorter than the other, Tom wore a built-up boot, and after Dominic and my Dad had gone back to the café, I sat and watched him hirple between his bench and lathe, muttering, holding the new thing up to the light. Handles twirled on and off, the lathe whirred, filings blew away, minute measurements were made with a micrometer, and a new bit for the shiny paddle began to take shape. I was mesmerised.

By 10 a.m. Forte's café was filling up and Tom and my Dad were 'faking something up, Dominic, just a lash-up'. It worked. An hour later fresh ice-cream came out of the spin-drier, the sun beat down, the Sunday queue formed and 'Jackie, Jackie, Tom, you never pay here. You and the boy never pay. Never.'

The daily delivery vans brought out housewives in Inchmead Drive, my Gran and a gaggle of kids, who enjoyed a golden chance to misbehave, for no-one went back indoors with their floury paper bags or cardboard cake cartons until all the formalities of the blether, the weather and the Wide World had been comprehended. Jock Trummle's real name was Turnbull, a characteristic metathesis made by country people and something that seemed somehow to describe a bond of familiarity between him and my Gran. Jock gave me bags of broken biscuits and crumpled hazel cakes. He liked my Gran and so he liked me.

Every day the vans brought bulletins, news from the Wide World, from places far beyond the fences, from places needing boldness to explore, and a blind eye from Bina. Like a morbid magnet it was death that drew me out of the safety of the back garden and down to the bottom of our street. Inchmead Drive is a cul-de-sac stopended by a high wall, and behind the high wall stood the Victorian mass of the Poorhouse, the place where old people were taken to end their days. And when they were dead, their dead bodies were laid out in the Morgue. And the roof of the Morgue was just visible over the high wall where the Poorhouse precinct bordered the land of the living and the rugby ground. How I came to understand this piece of the geography of the Wide World has vanished from memory. Perhaps Bina threatened me with the Poorhouse when my swearing became too experimental.

Much too high and smooth-sided to climb, the wall forbad direct access to the inner courtyard of the Poorhouse and the Morgue, but to the left was a wicket gate opening on to a short path which led past some old pigsties and through a door in the wall. One morning Mrs Newton chased me out of the garden, but despite incidental threats and harassment I could see that the problem was fundamental. It was possible to slip unnoticed into the Poorhouse grounds, but if you were seen and pursued, how did you get out if you were not near the door in the wall? What prompted these thoughts was more than a childish imitation of the military jargon I picked up from war comics: Battler Britton or Commando, or Biggles and Ginger who were always going on recces. (How did you say that? Ressies? Rekess? Recks?) Basically I wanted to sneak into the Poorhouse without being detected and see a real dead person, perhaps even touch them, and get away with it.

But how to gain entrance to the Morgue itself? There was bound to be a dead body in it, for according to Bina and the housewives out at the delivery vans, all that ever happened in the Wide World was death or serious illness. It seemed that in Kelso people were dropping like flies. But how to get to see a stiff and escape detection? No-one had ever sighted the matron of the Poorhouse, and even if she was less terrifying than Hattie

Jacques, she must still be terrifying. Matrons just were. What would happen if I got caught? No chance of a rescue from Bina. She'd never make it in her slippers and anyway she herself had a mortal dread of the Poorhouse. Would the police take my name and then tell Dad who would belt me? Colin Purves had really caught it for stealing apples. That was bad, but it was OK bad. What if in the Poorhouse there were small rooms without windows where nameless people were kept for years, after they had been apprehended while wandering around inside the high walls? How could anyone hear you shouting for help in the little rooms? Bina said that once you went into the Poorhouse you never came out again.

Eventually curiosity waxed stronger than fear and while my Gran was snoring and whiffling in her chair, the *Weekly Journal* having slid to the floor, I stole out of the back door and ran the fifty yards to the wicket gate. Without stopping I barged through the door in the wall and round the corner of the Poorhouse to see that the Morgue was a small building standing by itself. The door handle turned and I was inside. In the Morgue. With the dead people. It was black-dark with no windows and I could see nothing as I stood panting with my back to the door. Very slowly ghostly shapes emerged from the gloom and it turned out that there was a window in one wall whose panes had been painted over. I could see a row of tables that must have been used for slabs and on one of them there was a long rectangular sheet spread over a shape. A shape. But before another thought could spark, something in me snapped, and my courage evaporated. I pulled open the door into the blinding sunshine and ran for my life out of the Poorhouse.

Perhaps if I had been in less of a hurry to escape from the Morgue I might have noticed a wooden sign by the door that read 'Laundry'. When I skidded back in the back door of 42, Gran was still snoring.

The morbid shadow of the Morgue loomed in my imagination but it paled beside the raw and real fear that pursued me on many journeys through the Wide World. Mabel Woodhead reigned as matriarch over the childhood terror across the road at 29 Inchmead Drive. For many months her sons, Ernest, Norman and Arthur Woodhead, and their dog, laid ambushes, took turns to lay into me while their brothers held my arms and once even tried (unsuccessfully) to persuade the bemused dog to pee on me while I was pinned to the ground. Even roaring her loudest and waving her stick, Bina was too slow and too far away to help me. And passers-by mostly ignored the screaming and swearing. On her way home from the office Miss Cassie once stepped elegantly through the fracas on the pavement, but sometimes a barked admonition from a group of stern men in overalls coming up home from their work bought me enough time to flee back to the sanctuary of No. 42.

'He has to fight his own battles,' was my Dad's tight-lipped reaction when my Gran retailed the latest massacre. If I managed occasionally to draw a little blood from an isolated Norman or Arthur (Ernest was older and much tougher), Mabel would march across to 42 and bang on the front door. And when Bina or my Ma tried to cut short her rant by shutting the door in her face, she shoved her foot in to stop them. But such solidarity amongst the Woodheads failed to move my Dad. It didn't matter that Mabel wholeheartedly supported her sons in any circumstance, because in no circumstance would he intervene to support his. When my Dad wanted to teach me how to swim he took a direct approach, and as I tried to wriggle out of his grip, he threw me into the sea. It was the same with the Woodheads: a misconceived notion of the process of natural selection. I still panic in deep water, can barely swim and hate to have water near my mouth or nose.

Exploration may have been inhibited by the terror at No. 29, but it still went on. Several times I slipped past the sentries and gained the freedom of the Wide World. Cobey, Bindie McCombie, Colin Purves, Bob Thomson and I managed to muster enough daring between us to venture beyond Inchmead

Drive, sometimes all the way up the Meadows. Too steep for housing or cultivation, this broad area of whins, elder, hawthorn and rabbit warrens ran along the rim of the flood plain and allowed long prospects over Kelso to the banks of the Tweed, and beyond to the folded ridges in the south and even unimaginably far to the hazy heads of the Cheviots and the border with darkest England. This was geography on an epic scale and entirely beyond the ken or comprehension of Cobey, Bindie, Colin, Bob or me.

The battlefields of Europe were much closer to home, for what made the Meadows exciting was war. Crawling on our elbows through the long grass, darting with our rifles between clumps of whin bushes, and charging, yelling down the slope, we re-enacted the Second World War most afternoons. Only eight or nine years after the fall of the Third Reich, this was no imaginative game, but recent and vivid history. Most men wore bits of old army uniform to their work: khaki battledress jackets in summer and black berets and greatcoats in winter, and carried their sandwich tins and thermoses jammed into old gasmask bags. Everyone had seen their Dad's medals and it was clearly understood that, distributed amongst HM forces' crack regiments, Kelso men had been largely responsible for defeating Hitler. Sort of like Battler Britton, Eck Leid had probably swung the Normandy landings in the Allies' favour, Jinx Thomson the barber had a pivotal role at Monte Cassino and the Japs had been chased all the way back to Tokyo by Doddie Wood, with the assistance of a few others, mainly men from Jedburgh, Galashiels and Hawick. We had even seen and been allowed to touch a real German helmet and heard stories of tremendous trophies brought back in triumph to Kelso after our town defeated the Wehrmacht. And in Inchmead Drive, at No. 18, lived a real German. Except for his accent, Herman Triebel was disconcertingly normal, and he had probably not been a Panzer general, a member of the Gestapo or Hitler's right-hand man. And probably didn't keep a luger hidden in the coalbox. 'Never seen it, honest,' shrugged his son, Ralph, while undergoing interrogation.

While the terrain of the Meadows was perfect for infantry battles (until the pram wheels were attached to Cobey's bogey, we had no motorised armour), our problems lay in the rules of engagement. Naturally the Germans always lost, but how exactly? Using sticks of approximately the right shape and making satisfactory guttural gunfire noises, we mowed down the hordes of Huns from the Wehrmacht, but how did you know your invisible bullets had hit their targets unless the opposition agreed to a dramatic death while the bullet was speeding on its deadly way? There was a limit to the number of times Ralph Triebel would scream, clutch his chest and fall into a whin bush. If we made him do it too often, he just went home for his tea.

These problems were never resolved. But Berlin still fell to the indomitable courage of a gang of charging and whooping children from Kelso. 'Take that, you filthy Hun!' When news of our unstoppable advance filtered through to German High Command, there was panic. '*Gott im Himmel*, ze Scottish *schweinhunds* from Kelso!' Eventually Hitler was forced to bow to the inevitable and took to his bunker. And since most of us had a bunker outside the back door (regularly topped up by visiting Africans), we knew that this really was the end for the Führer, a crouching, coal-blackened stroke of profound ignominy for the Leader of the Third Reich.

Perhaps inspired by his example or, more likely, by those intrepid Kelso men who escaped from prisoner-of-war camps, we became keen tunnellers. Under the old turf, the Meadows had sandy, stoneless soil and it was easy to dig out but sufficiently compacted not to cave in, much. Tunnels became dens and many acquired earth ramparts at the entrance, sometimes augmented by bits of wooden crates or old fencing. Others burrowed deep into the hillside, turned sideways and out again at a separate entrance. Sometimes the bigger tunnels collapsed but such was their scale that no-one temporarily buried seemed to panic or be hurt. When the dens were complete they were usually quickly abandoned. That is because their main attraction was the process of creation. Once a den had been tunnelled out, what was there to do? Just sit in it for a while, feel like you were in hiding, in your own place. Once when we saw Frank Hawker and his black leather gang walk menacingly across Croft Park, we all scuttered into our den like startled rabbits. But that was the only time it was used as a refuge. Dens were good for the secret storage of contraband and since none of ours was ever valuable, it was safe there. No-one could be bothered to steal our collection of sheep skulls, interesting stones, a tin bucket with a hole in the bottom or a piece of old pram harness that Cobey found and swore was from a German paratrooper his Dad had strangled.

Matches, however, were extremely valuable, and required to be stolen with great care. That usually meant no box to strike them on, which in turn needed even more care, particularly when it was windy. A striking stone and some dry grass was the most reliable method to get a fire going, but that sometimes meant holding on to the match until it burned your fingers. Bindie McCombie yelped, threw away what he thought was a spent match and nearly burnt down the Meadows once when the wind blew his grass fire across the slope like the spreading red edges of a black carpet. We all stood and gawped in open-mouthed horror before deciding unanimously to blame Bindie if it came to a long stretch in prison. He burst into tears, howled the place down. But the fire ran out of dry grass and smoked to a halt before it reached the Ash Path.

The Abbotseat Gang waited and watched. Chipper MacKay, Deggy Laidlaw, Pete Gillespie, Chick Gleed and their troops knew that we were on their territory, but they also realised that if they approached too close, they would end up in the dock with Bindie, facing the consequences, whoever they were. From up on the Meadows all the gang territories in Kelso were visible. Immediately below roamed the Croft Road Gang with Peeny MacLeod, his big brother Tam and Ritchie Playfair. Nearer the river lay the domain of the Roxburgh Street Arabs, but they were said to be more interested in exploring the forbidden vastness behind the Duke's Dykes than bothering us up at the Meadows. But between Roxburgh Street and Croft Road lay the land of darkness, the lair of the most terrifying presence (not many had seen him, and Cobey's claim to have said hello once was never believed), the place where The Most Dangerous Man in Kelso lived. In Orchard Park dwelt Zeke Lillie. He was so bad that nobody knew what he had done.

Bindie, Bob, Colin, Cobey and I were too few and too little to be a gang. No Big Boys lived down our end of Inchmead Drive and the only remote possibility of leadership, the red-haired Twinny Todds, actually lived in Inchmead Crescent and anyway had understandings with the Croft Road Gang. When gang fights threatened to rumble across the Meadows, we all sat up at the top field fences, well out of the way, watched and were glad to be nothing more than the audience. Mostly gang fights in Kelso consisted only of menacing manoeuvres and some imaginative insults, but when the cops did come once, we scattered like all the others, hiding in an air-raid shelter in the fields near the golf course.

'Where the bloody hell have you been?' My Dad's first smack knocked me sideways. 'Your Mother, your Grannie and I have been out looking for you, worried to bloody death!' And then the hammering I got was followed by 'Straight to bed, no bloody tea for you!' I managed to hold back the howl until I got behind the bedroom door where I could safely let out the whole snotty, explosive lot. In Inchmead Drive a belting from your Dad was common, but not getting your tea was a cruel and unusual punishment, particularly since I was starving that night.

Ernest Woodhead and I were enjoying a rare truce and he wanted to do something dangerous, as usual. And for once so did I. Perhaps I thought whatever it was would make me as tough as Ernie, my temporary and dangerous friend. Beyond the Meadows lay the Big House. Broomlands was screened from a view of the town and the council estate by a thick belt of tall hardwood trees and tangles of rhododendrons. Perfect cover. And between the trees and the Big House was a wide area of open parkland punctuated by solitary trees fenced against grazing animals. Perfect cover if you were quick.

The point of Ernie's expedition was never explained. True hard men didn't talk, they grunted, flicked their heads and eyes sideways in a certain direction or sometimes resorted to a variety of hand-signals to indicate halt, keep quiet or freeze. So far as I could make out, the idea was to get as close as possible to the Big House without being detected. A sort of architectural tig. Jeopardy was supplied by the baillies, and if one of them caught you, you couldn't sit down for a week. And then they told your Dad so that you got a second leathering. The Duke's water-baillies were even more terrifying. If they saw you inside the Duke's Dykes around Floors Castle and thought you might be poaching salmon from the Tweed, they kicked your arse, told your Dad, and then told the police as well, who took your name down before they came round to the front door in full view of all the neighbours to deliver a black affront. And then Ma and Bina glowered while Dad belted me again. 'Have you had enough now?' What sort of a question was that? I never wanted any.

That August night Ernie and I crept through the rhododendra, dropped down the ha-ha wall into the parks around Broomlands and risked all in a daring zig-zag manoeuvre between the fenced trees. Nothing stirred in the Big House. No 'Hey! What do think you're at?' Instead I was seized with a sudden and urgent need, probably related to the green plums we had pinched from the walled garden. Ernie must have shaken his head at the shame of it. How could I run with my shorts round my ankles, and if I got caught in the act, the baillies would have left a tattoo of tackits on my backside.

When we regained the safety of Inchmead Drive, thunder clouds had gathered over No. 42, and my Dad let me have it.

Over at 29 Ernie probably got a medal, as well as his tea. After the rumble of anger around the living room had subsided I heard Gran climbing the stairs. Because of her 'pains', she had to negotiate each tread on all fours and the signature puffing and creaking was unmistakable. She brought me drop-scones hidden in her apron and a cuddle.

Perhaps because of the black affront of the Broomlands expedition, the shame of having to ask neighbours and passers-by if they had seen her grandson, Bina began to drag me along with her when she went out to see her friends. These were outings only undertaken in dry, settled weather, for the sake of Bina's slippers. She moved so slowly along Inch Road, one hand on the dyke by the horsefield, the other gripping a thick butter-coloured walking stick which was also handy for poking at objects of interest noted on the way or for wielding at me if my impatience began to fray into ill nature. Inching along the Inch, shuffling in her slippers, stopping to speak to bloody everybody, Bina and I were bound for Addie Scott's house in Inch Park. It was different, huge, not a council house but one half of a substantial villa in a street of semi-detached houses down one side and low-rise council flats down the other. No-one ever used Addie Scott's front door. Bina and I shuffled round to the back porch and into the kitchen.

I stuck close to my Gran for Addie Scott was terrifying, even when she meant to be ordinary. Tall like Bina and with her hair cut short and crimped at the edges, she had a large port-wine stain on one cheek. It made her look permanently angry, and her natural abruptness seemed aggressive when it was mostly only practical. But Bina liked her and they could talk for hours while I wandered around the vast house, pushing my fingers through the holes in the lace tablecloth in the dark front room.

Addie Scott was a woman of mystery. Her husband was Wilson Simpson the chimneysweep but even he didn't have enough surnames to give one to his wife. And even more mysterious, Addie's children had different names! Rae Scott (a woman), Ally Simpson (a man) and Dave Simpson (another man). How did all this happen? There was a confusing habit in Kelso of continuing to label married women with their maiden names, or at least the names they had before they got married to their present husbands, those still living, that is. I think. Ruth Barnes walked down Inchmead Drive every weekday to her work and was never called anything else, even though her husband was definitely Mr Todd the insuranceman. I think. But how did Rae Scott, daughter of Addie Scott, keep her surname when Wilson Simpson had so many to spare? Bina would never explain. It was all just part of the world of adults, a remote region of the past to which children were never to be admitted. Perhaps the passwords were too complicated, perhaps Addie Scott's glare was guardian enough of something that was nobody else's business, perhaps it was the beginning of forgetting. If it was, then it worked, for I was never told that story, lost the wish to know it, only remembered the questions.

My Grannie had come to live with us in 1952. She had suffered a mild heart attack, but even though the doctor had said it was nothing much to worry about if she would only lose some weight, my Dad insisted that she move into our new council house at 42. Although three bedrooms seemed like a luxury after our prefab, when my younger sister was born, I had to sleep with my Gran. I was four and by coincidence I have a photo taken at that time – no doubt the camera came out to take a birthday snap of my baby sister. I remember the day well. My Ma must have been out to work because my Gran fussed about the house all day, straightening things that were already straight, making first day kail (it was November), and every time she passed me, she licked the palm of her hand and tried to flatten my cow's lick hair. Finally exasperated at its defiance, she announced that she would find the clippers and give me a haircut. After a lot of rummaging in the sideboard drawers (an indelible detail – even though we never had any, there was always a whiff of cigars when these were pulled open), she advanced on me with intent. Lifting me up under the oxters on to the draining board, she set about my spiky coif. After twenty minutes of tugging and tearing at my hair to the accompaniment of screaming and swearing (I was always a grand swearer) and wriggling, she finally let me down. Her handiwork is on celluloid. As a child I had chipmunk cheeks and a ba' heid underlined by a spectacular pet lip, depending on the occasion. My Gran had left me with a very short back and sides and most of the top had been felled as well. Only my cow's lick remained. I looked like a bad-tempered, badly shawed turnip, reacting to invisible threats with a sickly camera smile.

When bedtime came I was roared upstairs into Grannie's bed. Our house had no heating outside the living room, and hopping from foot to foot on the freezing linoleum, I threw off my outer clothes and pulled pyjamas over my vest and pants. Sometimes my Ma would put a hot water pig in the bed to take the chill off the sheets. A pottery version of a hot water bottle, the pig sometimes scalded an incautious foot. The trick was to get near enough to feel its glow and arrange the bedclothes to allow some convection to rise up and warm where you lay. So that my Gran didn't wake me when she came up, the bedside light was left on. I remember a still life on the nightstand: a quarter-bottle of Martell brandy secured with a metal clip stopper (this was to ease Gran's pains), a copy of one of the works of Annie S. Swan or O. Henry, a tumbler for her teeth and a hairbrush. When Gran undid her bun, she let down long and luxuriant black hair with only a fleck or two of grey. Out of sight under the bed was a chamber pot, and the tinkling sound of its use often punctuated the night.

My Grannie's bed seemed huge and had a horsehair mattress which crackled when I turned over. The springs were loose and the whole structure impossibly flimsy and possibly capable of dynamic movement. Crackling was sometimes supplemented by the squeal of complaining metal: frame, bedsprings, headboard. Sometimes I thought the bed might begin to purr like an engine, lift itself off the linoleum and fly through the windows into the night sky. When Gran came to bed I always woke up. She was about four times my weight and the effect of her getting under the blankets and quilts was to topple me into the deep dent she had moulded into the horsehair. Determined not to end up nestling against her soft warm volume (cuddling like a wee lassie would) and not liking the mixture of camphor and oldness she smelt of, I clung like a sleepy limpet to the edge of the mattress. But I remember the warmth Bina radiated in the wintertime; it seemed to wrap around me, made me feel like a bear cub in a winter cave. And sometimes she scratched my back to soothe me.

As my grip on the mattress loosened Bina told me stories, hundreds of stories, most of them lost on the edges of sleep. Our heads lay one behind the other on a long bolster pillow, and while she whispered, I watched the moon rise through the window. Once when she was an upstairs maid at Floors Castle, her job had been to set and light the fires very early in the morning. That meant she was the only person up, walking through the dark, empty state-rooms. One solitary morning, when the snow was on the ground and the moon glinted off the winter fields, she swore to me that she had seen a ghost. A tiny pinprick of light shone away down across the castle lawns at the edge of the River Tweed. Gradually it began to move until it swept up the slope to the French windows my Gran stood at. It was an old woman in a white nightgown and with white hair. And she reached out a gossamer hand to touch my Gran's face through the panes. Did I dream the last part?

Another night she told me something equally memorable about her other jobs at Floors. She claimed that when the toffs went to the lavatory, they did not use prickly pine Izal toilet roll or squares of newspaper like everybody else. Every morning my Grannie had to wash the used linen napkins from the day before.

When I was old enough to begin to ask questions about her young life, she always answered with a story. Even if it wandered and never reached the point of my original enquiry, I didn't mind. Bina told good tales.

A bit later, when she had finally got me expelled from her bed for kicking during the night, I asked about something which had been puzzling me. My Mother came from a big family in Hawick and I had dozens of cousins, aunts, and uncles there. But none in Kelso. None at all.

'Aye well, son,' she said, looking away out of the window, 'it was the War. A lot of people never came back.'

And then she embarked on a story about a neighbour, Dand Elliot, when he was on National Service in Hong Kong. Walking along a main thoroughfare on a beautiful sunny morning he spied, to his astonishment, a man from Kelso coming towards him head and shoulders above the bustle of Chinese. It was Bertie Wardlaw, an eccentric proto-hippy much given to seasonal work and seasonal travelling. 'Aye Dand, grand morning,' he said walking straight past, without breaking his stride.

My Grannie always sat by the living room window unashamedly staring at everyone who went past. People on their way to work often waved and she waved back. I never thought anything of it. Bina Moffat was so old, if I ever considered it at all, that she probably knew everybody in Kelso. If a stranger did happen by, she would whip round and snap at me playing on the floor: 'Quick, who's that?' I almost never knew.

Like most old women in those days long ago, when these things really mattered, her immediate reaction to hearing of new people was to try to fit them somehow into her genealogical jigsaw. Often she tried several connections before she made the right one.

'Now that's her that's married on the postman at Sprouston.' A pause that could last half an hour. 'No, no, no,' she would say in the middle of a TV programme everybody else was watching, 'Stichill, aye Stichill, the postman at Stichill. That's her.'

When repeated attempts at a genealogical context failed, the unknown person in question was consigned, with a sigh, to a limbo where the unattached wandered aimlessly. 'Just cannot make her into anybody.'

My sisters teased her, once saying that they had met Sean Connery buying a pie in Scott the Bakers in Roxburgh Street. 'Now, that's him that's married on the minister's daughter at Maxton.' A short pause 'No, no, no. Mertoun. Aye, that's right, Mertoun.' No, Gran. He's a film star, you know, James Bond. 'Aye well, he's done very well for himself then, has he not?'

Later I tried again to get Gran to unpack our family's genealogy, our relations and not those of people who passed the living room window.

'If your name is Moffat, like me and Dad, what was your maiden name then?'

I remember this disconcerted her and she blustered a bit before saying, 'Jeffrey, it was Jeffrey,' and then returned to her watching vigil by the window without another word.

TWO

In the Dream Time

THE SNOW ALWAYS brought stillness behind it. By the time the last of the flakes had settled on Inchmead Drive, it was gloaming and the quiet was everywhere. At the upstairs bedroom window, looking down on the street below, I was waiting, craning to see, rubbing breath-mist off the panes, waiting for him to come. Opposite 42 Inchmead Drive stood a lamppost, and in the early dark of the winter, the leerie came to light it. With a long pole he hooked open the little glass door, swivelled the top to light the gas and spill a yellow glow across to our house. When it snowed the leerie crunched his way from one lamppost to the next, dropping pools of gold up the grey and white street. It was a cold night, ice crystals sparkled on the window panes and the snow would definitely stay until the morning.

Cobey's had flaps folded like spaniel's ears, Bindie wore something like a teacosy and Bina had knitted me one so big it had a breastplate down to my waist. The opening at the front of my balaclava was so small and the fit so tight that my eyebrows seemed almost to touch my bottom lip. In the hall mirror I looked like a bad-tempered miniature old man, stiff with layers of clothing, a mitten on each hand and my trousers stuffed into thick socks and shoved into wellies. In the Three Stooges the one with the weird page-boy haircut used to knit his brows, pout, and then shake his jowls before bopping the bald one. My face appeared to have frozen in a similar scowl. I couldn't shake anything, and in fact if I turned too quickly, I might have slid round inside the balaclava, leaving an ear to stick out of the hole, and find myself sideways on to my coat buttons.

When Bina was finally satisfied that I would be warm enough, she opened the front door of 42 and the blinding white world screwed up my screwed-up eyes even more. The snow was deep, and on the untouched front green nearly up to the top of my wellies. None of us had sledges, but Cobey's Dad had given him a big steel tray from his chip van. And once we were round the corner, out of sight of Bina or anybody else's Ma, we tore off the balaclavas and stuffed them in a coat pocket for when it got even colder. And mittens? Nobody could make a proper snowball with mittens on and they came off as soon as we reached the Poorhouse dyke, where snow was at a handy height.

Because it was so different from the day before, everywhere was interesting. The snow had discouraged what traffic there was and on Cobey's tray we could sledge down the slope at the foot of Forestfield and right out on to Inch Road. As the surface compacted and slippery patches shone in the tracks we made, the tray slithered all the way across the road and down the gentle incline past Bindie's house. Snowbound in her slippers at 42, Bina would never venture outside in weather like this and all sorts of reckless freedoms beckoned.

Up at the Double Bump, big boys with proper sledges flew down from the edge of the fields above the Meadows. Some of them began by running, pushing their sledges, legs bicycling behind before flopping on only yards before the first of the Bumps, a footpath cut into the hillside. Not many came off there, but most did at the second. How the few sledgers who managed to stay on absorbed the bone-jarring impact on their rib-cages and pelvises seemed to me, then and now, a matter of mysterious bravery. The majority who parted company with their sledges often hit the soft snow to the sides of the Double

Bump run, but for the more adhesive the track had become like icy white concrete. Some who completed the run slowed themselves, using their toes to steer and brake, and got up off their sledges very carefully. Occasionally there was Technicolor drama in the white landscape. Blood, vivid red blood, spattered the snow when one of the Roxburgh Street Arabs bashed his nose against something hard. Cobey, Bindie, Bob, Colin and I just stood at the top and watched, waiting to be Big Boys.

Balaclavas made you feel like a deep-sea diver, observing the world from inside something, not part of it. But together with the layers of clothing that allowed a slow, stiff-legged and stiff-armed walk, they were an excellent disguise. And an excellent disguise was absolutely necessary to go out on the ice of the frozen river. At the Cobby, Tweed was wide and deep, and deadly. Anyone who fell through a hole in the ice would be instantly sucked under by the swirling currents and drowned, chilled to a gasping death in the milky darkness below the frozen sheets. All of us had been told often, given a real telling, fingers wagged in our faces, that we were never, ever to go on the ice when the River Tweed was frozen over. So, of course, at the first opportunity we did exactly that, drawn to mortal danger like metal to a magnet. After Bindie got a terrible doing for walking on the ledge on the outside of the parapet of Kelso Bridge, sixty feet up, nothing between him and the surging river below, we all did it the day after. Cobey with no hands.

When we had frog-marched our way from the Double Bump to the frozen Tweed, it seemed that everybody in Kelso had failed to take a telling and decided, as a community, to risk death by going on the ice. Dr Davidson and his friends had marked out a curling rink and even lit a brazier to warm themselves. We were amazed that nobody had noticed the pooling riverwater underneath it, but when Bindie inadvertantly walked across the rink, only just noticing a grey stone with a handle on it slithering towards him, Dr Davidson roared at us. Scary, with a startling glass eye, permanent five o'clock shadow and a gruff manner, he scattered us like a blatter of pigeons and we skittered into the middle of the river. Where we stopped, paralysed by fright, remembering the doomladen tellings, never having intended to come this far out. No-one dared breathe as we listened for cracks and groans under our feet.

'Sweep! Sweep!' shouted one of the skips at the curling rink, and we all jumped. Colin was the skinniest, the least likely to fall through a patch of thin ice, at least not all the way through. And despite his clingy diffidence, we all thought it was best that he went first, was the Leader of the Expedition, like Captain Scott, or Battler Britton, anybody really brave we could think of. But which way? Bob Thompson needed a pee (how he would find anything to pee with under all his coats and jumpers was not something that occurred to anyone) and anyway it was far too dangerous to splash hot and yellow pee on the fragile ice. None of us had ever walked on the water before and the view from the middle of the Tweed was so unfamiliar as to be disorienting. Did the Fairgreen bank look closer than the town bank? Definitely maybe. Cobey shoved Colin towards the Fairgreen and we were off, a terrified crocodile of unwilling polar explorers, bound for uninhabited regions, far from help, with only penguins for company. Possibly.

Colin gasped and stopped suddenly, the rest of us concertina-ing in behind him like The Three Stooges. We were only a few yards from what appeared to be the Fairgreen bank, and the ice had stopped. The white-out of the snow had fooled us into approaching not the riverbank but the steep, cascading weir just in front of it where part of the Tweed's flow rushed down to join the Teviot at the Junction Pool. We all stared at the edge of the ice and the water gushing out from underneath it. No-one moved. If we ever get out of this alive, I promised God and Bina, I will never, ever swear again on a Sunday or pick my nose even if I'm sure nobody is looking.

'All right there boys!' With his hands clasped behind his back, trouser-bottoms tucked into his socks and wearing a jaunty cut hat, The Skater scraped up to us, spraying ice everywhere and stopping dead by digging in a metal toe. 'Don't you go too close now.' He had started moving again, circling us slowly, hypnotically. 'Not deep there, but very, very cold.' The Skater looked a bit like a tramp, with a length of twine tied around his waist to stop his jacket from flapping open. He smiled at us, and moving gracefully from side to side ploughed away upstream towards Floors Castle. And then, as our jaws dropped, he suddenly turned around and kept going in the same direction, but backwards, with his hands still behind his back. The world seemed to shift on its axis, Bob Thompson nearly peed himself and Cobey tried skating in his wellies.

Dr Davidson's brazier was beginning to glow brighter as the sun dipped behind the trees on the Fairgreen. And after a snowball fight on the road up home, we came to the igloo in the horsefield. Cobey, Bob Thompson and Bindie all lived next door to each other, directly opposite the horsefield, and they could keep several eyes on the igloo, watching out for gangs of Big Boys who might want to kick it down on their way home from the chip shop. Or maybe Zeke Lillie would cast his fell shadow over it. There was only room in the igloo for two at a time (bigger igloos kept collapsing) and one of them always had to be Bindie because it was his job to steal the matches. And the other always had to be Cobey because the candle was his. So that we could all feel like Eskimos around a campfire (where did they get the wood?) Colin, Bob and I pulled on our balaclavas and sat around the entrance hole as it got darker. It shouldn't have been a hole but a small tunnel, like in Cobey's comic, but that kept collapsing as well. Wet on the outside after the snowball fight and wet on the inside after sweating under the weight of so much clothing, we began to feel the cold for the first time. Bob had a runny nose which had begun to turn the bottom part of his balaclava into a sheet of snotty ice. And after some discussion, with plenty of pauses for thought, of how far south polar bears ventured in the winter (nobody believed Cobey when he said he'd seen one, honest, up at the Meadows), we put out the precious candle, trudged over the horsefield, climbed the fence and went home for our tea. And for the routine enquiries. As she hung up my sodden clothes on the clothes-horse to steam in front of the fire, Bina tutted and shook her head. She never believed anything I told her, even when it was occasionally true.

Winters were the dream time, the dark nights so long and heavy and full of unconscious incident. Mostly I dreamed about furniture, the menacing furniture crammed into Bina's bedroom: a chest of drawers with barley-sugar pillars that swivelled and squeaked as they turned up into infinity, a tallboy with metal handles that rattled and a built-in press with a suction hiss when its doors were opened. In the galaxies behind my closed eyelids, the chest expanded, grew so enormous, the size of a coal lorry, that it squashed me up against the rattling tallboy, threatening to impale me on its vicious handles. And all the time the world turned like a waltzer at the shows, a brass band played oompah music and Bina's room flew past the winter moon into outer space. No matter which way I twisted, or how small I made myself, the window or the door to the landing were always too far away to reach. And my skin felt cold, and it seemed as though my back pressed constantly against an invisible knife-edge. The air was prickly with needles, growing ever more humid, so humid that I couldn't breathe any more.

It was always the same when Bina woke me. Under the great weight of blankets and quilts my pyjamas were soaked with sweat, and sometimes with pee. 'Over to my side, wee lamb,' as she rolled me into her warm, deep dent, after stripping off the sodden nightclothes. And it was warm after the cold dreams in outer space, so snug that I pulled my knees up into a curl, tucked the covers up to my chin and sleepily watched Bina pull off the single sheet she always put on my side.

'If you look at it long enough,' she whispered to me one cloudless night, 'you can see the old moon in the shadow of the new.' As the curved silver sliver grew into a crescent and brightened, I wondered what Bina meant. Was the thickening crescent another moon, a different one covering over the old one? Did it look the same in Australia? Could they see round behind it? Our heads on the bolster pillow, hers behind mine, cuddled into her warmth, staring out of the bedroom window at the night sky, I tried to understand, asking her often where the new moon came from, and why the dead moon hid in its shadow. Did it turn when the world turned? 'That's just how things happen,' was all she would say, staring with me up at its milky brilliance. When I was a little boy I thought of it as Bina's moon, and sometimes when I see it rise over the wood below my house, the old woman's words come whispering back to comfort me in the stillness of a winter night.

If it fell on a weekday, my Dad wasn't at home on Christmas Day. He was at work, because until television and commerce combined to produce a nationwide demand, Christmas was barely noticed in 1950s Scotland. But my Ma liked it and always took a day off. Even though it was generally seen as a very English festival when God rested Merry Gentlemen, who looked like John Bull on a John Bull printing set, and dozens of mufflered English people sang carols in snowy English villages lit by lamps on long sticks, my Ma enthusiastically adopted as many of its traditions as didn't cost any money. And she wholeheartedly embraced the smiling spirit of Christmas. I think she liked that it seemed to revolve around children, families, gifts, and was a splash of welcome colour in the depths of a dreich and grey winter. New Year was celebrated in Scotland with a universal holiday and a great deal of gusto and cheer, but it was for adults, and it centred around the business of getting drunk, having licence to behave badly once a year, the night generally coming to an end when a reveller passed out, or foundered, like a ship coming aground on the rocks.

In the cupboard under the stairs, right at the back, behind

Bina's sewing basket, was the box full of 'decs', the shorthand my Ma used for the Christmas decorations. There was tinsel, coloured ribbon, a wooden Santa in his sleigh, and a big star covered with silver paper for the top of the tree. But what Ma liked best was the bunting strung from the centre light fitting to each corner of the living room. One year Barbara, Marjie, Ma and I made coloured paper-chains with scissors and messy Gloy glue, while Bina sewed the cardboard Santa back on to the blue and red concertinas of stiff paper which were pinned to the pelmet above the window.

In the woods up at Broomlands and on the road round the Hendersyde Estate we went on holly-gathering expeditions with Ma and a pair of Dad's snips from his toolbox. 'Always get a bit with berries, berries bring you luck.' And we always got a bit without berries to tie on Joey the Budgie's cage. They might have poisoned him. While the crinkly, prickly holly leaves stayed green until after New Year, the berries seemed to disappear gradually until there were none left. Perhaps we were running out of luck, perhaps they fell off, or perhaps Bina fed them quietly to the bloody budgie.

Each Christmas Ma began to spend a few pennies on the decs, particularly for the tree. We had good lights which Dad rigged up so that some stayed on all the time and the ones at the top could flash on and off if you wanted them to. Bina didn't want them to, but the soft glow of a Christmas tree's lights always brought a smile. It still does. We bought a set of crystal stars in a shop and improvised lots of new decs out of cardboard, with gold and silver paper. But one year Ma decided to splash out. We went down to Crosbie's the newsagent in Roxburgh Street and I was allowed to choose. My eyes widened at a small silver (plastic) trumpet. It was magical, beautiful, perfect in every little detail, with the shape of the valves picked out and what looked just like a tiny mouthpiece. Having refused to let Ma put it in a paper bag and carry it with the rest of her shopping, I had to have it to myself, there and then. Walking up the busy pavement

I tried to blow into the miniature trumpet, blew it out of my grasp, and a man stood on it.

Dazed with shock I gazed at the shattered fragments before an ear-splitting wail burst out of me. All in a moment tragedy had followed upon joy and the perfect silver trumpet was reduced to irrevocable, ungluable smithereens by a passer-by who had no idea what he had done. The man just kept on walking, oblivious to the heartbreak collapsing into a mother's skirts behind him.

One Christmas Santa came to the Store, the Kelso Co-operative and Wholesale Society, Hardware Department, Second Floor. Perhaps because he was stopping off on the way back to Lapland to load up, the Store Santa didn't have any presents. Or more likely it was because it wasn't Christmas Day yet, and he was really on a goodwill tour, not actually giving out presents yet, to anybody, but really just reassuring everybody that it would in fact be a very Merry Christmas. And that he really existed of course.

'Can't be reindeer.' Cobey was the first to wonder about practicalities, 'Seen him, never seen them. Have you?', and to worry about details: 'Don't have wings, do they?'

None of that was what bothered me about Santa, I just refused to sit on the man's knee, even if he really was who the manageress of the hardware department said he was. The summer before I had been scared all the way out of my wits by men dressed up in costumes. Standing on the pavement in Bowmont Street, minding my own business, working my way through a Lucky Bag from Donaldson's the grocer, I was suddenly roared and grunted at by four men dressed as cavemen, and then kidnapped by them. They were taking an over-enthusiastic part in Kelso's annual Fancy Dress Parade. Carried screaming to their prehistoric float, I was put in a wooden cage with another screaming child and a scatter of bloody bones from a butcher's shop. And it wasn't until Bina shoved her way through the crowd and banged on the lorry driver's cab with her stick that the cavemen let me out. Sobbing and shivering with fright, I was dragged back to 42 for some elderberry wine and a hazel cake.

And so the Store Santa waved at me from a safe distance, I nodded and Ma wondered why she had paid threepence. But Christmas morning never lost its magic. From the early hours, wrapped in quilts, Barbara, Marjie and I sat quiet at the top of the stairs waiting for the signal from Ma that Santa had been. You could tell he had come down the chimney because of the sooty fingerprints on his glass of milk and the presence of only crumbs on the plate where his slice of sponge cake had been. Cobey would have wondered how much cake one Santa could eat: forty-eight slices in Inchmead Drive alone. Perhaps he fed it to the reindeer, if they existed, that is.

When Ma finally came to the bottom of the stairs, she was almost knocked over by the stampede, while Bina's snoring was startled into a 'What in the name of God!?!' by the thunder of hoofbeats. Hanging from the mantlepiece where Mr Claus had munched his cake were three long stockings, and by the tree one present for each of us. These were almost always made by Dad; one year Marjie got a rocking crib for her dolly and I was given a garage made of blue-painted plywood with a sign on the front, 'Prop. A. Moffat'. In the toe of the stockings was a sixpence and a tangerine, and all sorts of other delights piled in after them: a chocolate Santa in red and white foil (peeled off carefully, it would make a dec for next Christmas), a bag of boiled sweets, a box of coloured wax Crayola crayons, a packet of Spangles, an eraser, a vile Brazil nut, a Lakeland pencil and sharpener, perhaps a small bag of marbles, perhaps a solid rubber ball with marbled whorls of red and blue swirling through it.

After an ignored breakfast and the departure of my Dad for his work, I went up to show Bina all the things Santa had brought (was he sort of the same as God?). She never gave presents herself until we were much older and Christmas more of an established holiday. And then they were usually socks or mittens she had made to replace the ones I lost every winter.

Down in the kitchen we helped Ma with the long preparation for Christmas dinner and I was sent out into the back garden to pick the frozen Brussels sprouts, snapping them off the thick stalks. Bina said they were peppery after a nip of frost. And then I wondered how many layers of little leaves a Brussels sprout could have before Ma showed me what to do and leave something for us to eat.

On the Scottish Home Service there were carols from an English church and Christmas messages for British Forces Overseas read out very slowly by a man with a voice like chocolate. His brother did the Pathé News at the Roxy. Ma liked the carols and sang along with them as she peeled potatoes to make those thick chips she coated with flour before frying them golden brown. Somewhere beyond the Meadows, the shepherds watched their flocks by night, while the Little Lord Jesus was asleep in the hay, once in Royal David's City, under yonder star, joyful and triumphant in Be-ethlehem, while for a few weeks God definitely became Santa, or the other way round.

·On the table we had candles and through the door only the glow of the Christmas tree lights in the living room. When Dad uncorked the first of his screwtops of India Pale Ale, we all waited, looking at Ma. She smiled, took some glasses, and with a tiny trickle of beer and a lot of lemonade she made us shandy. And then we all ate too much, even me.

Before television drew our eyes away from it, the fire was the focal point for most families on a winter's evening; perhaps the flames attracted us not just for the warmth but because they remembered an ancient sunshine stored for centuries in the coal and logs. After Christmas dinner, Dad, Ma and Bina settled into their easy chairs for forty winks at the hearthside, sometimes with the low murmur of the Light Programme in the background while we played in the glow. No-one told any stories that I can remember, not even Bina, but the dance of the firelight, the mesmeric flicker of yellow and blue seemed enough to content us, to put in the hours before bedtime.

New Year exploded the drowsy rhythms of the winter. There was no bedtime, at least not for adults, and on Old Year's Night, 31 December, our street was transformed into a thoroughfare of fun. What went on in the hours before and after the year's midnight was not something I ever saw when I was a little boy. But I heard it, and my imagination supplied the swaying, carousing, arm-round-the-shoulder images. On Old Year's Night we had a big dinner, bigger than at Christmas, and the chicken (Bina called it 'the brute') was always served with mashed potato. As though preparing for battle, my Dad insisted on 'lining your stomach' before a serious dram was taken. I was always in bed well before that happened, when the starting gun of midnight chimed and the taking of drams began in earnest. Moments later at No. 42 the doorbell rang, the door opened almost immediately, and the coming of the New Year was celebrated with the arrival of our first first-foot, usually a near neighbour. And for good luck, somebody dark was always preferred.

Later, voices I didn't recognise joined the party, sometimes a song woke me, the chorus swelling through the floorboards. And then the house seemed to empty and the gaggle and babble of conversation, the squeals and giggles and the occasional clink of a bottle would shift momentarily into the street before disappearing out of earshot into another house. What kept my attention was the business of straining to hear the range of what was said or sung. By turns, people seemed to shout and then lower their voices into a hushed whisper, and often they laughed.

The day after, New Year's Day, was much less raucous, much more indoors, and once, when my Dad came into the kitchen to refuse his breakfast on the morning after, his skin was tinged with green, like a potato left too long in the light. Partly out of wariness, partly out of curiosity I watched the adults who came to 42 on 1st January. Mostly they were women carrying small shopping bags full of small bottles: squat green gin with a white label and a metal clip top, tall brown port, whisky of all sorts and a bottle of plain lemonade. After the widespread failure of stomach lining to cope with the flow of too many drams the night before, men tended to stay at home on New Year's Day. Or if they were dragged out for the sake of an appearance, they sat quiet with a cup of tea and an ignored piece of black bun, nursing their heads while their wives enjoyed the small revenge with their dry sherry. Port and lemon, gin and It, even rum and pep, whisky and lemonade, eye-watering Crabbie's Green Ginger, shandy and other exotica lubricated conversation – often about the events of the night before. 'You know. He woke up. And. Looked straight at her. And said. Is it today or tomorrow? Well. I don't know.' As glasses were topped up and cigarettes lit, women sometimes became dangerously affectionate. But when I had positioned myself safely out of casual reach, I watched them, fascinated at how different New Year seemed to make them: louder certainly, emphatic and more deliberate, occasionally prone to blink very slowly while listening and nodding with a fixed lipstick smile.

Margaret Allen did none of these things, particularly not the listening. When she came to visit us at 42, her intelligence and vivacity extended beyond my Ma and Bina to encompass me and my sisters. Margaret talked to us like we were people, not brainless miniatures. And one New Year's Day she even brought us something to drink: Middlemas's lemonade, several varieties in little bottles called splits. Margaret worked at Middlemas's, in the flavour room where they mixed the right amounts of essence for each kind of lemonade. Dozens of different labels and colours rattled and clinked their way off the assembly line and into thick wooden crates: green Limeade, golden Cream Soda, clear and frothy American Cream Soda, red Kola, sticky red Cherryade, brilliant red Raspberryade, Ginger Beer that was cloudy like soapy water, green Appleade, green but vile Paletta and the eternal Plain Lemonade.

Before Margaret took us up to see the flavour room, I imagined lorryloads of cherries, limes, raspberries, kolas and palettas going down Distillery Lane to be made into juice at Middlemas's. But the prosaic reality was that Margaret, wearing a long

said. With me holding my nose, huffing and fidgeting by her side, Ma handed over the cash and her Divi Book to the manageress, took the bag unwrapped, and when we made it to the stairs to Crawford Street, we both gulped the fresh air.

Ma never liked the pedoscope, but it fascinated me. We were at the Store Footwear Department for school shoes, proper black lace-up, sensible shoes with leather uppers and a composition sole. 'Last forbloodyever if he'd only stop growing so bloody fast.' My Dad liked the principle of buying what he called the best of stuff: the problem was paying for it. Up until August 1955 I had run around happily in winter wellies and summer sandals, the sort with a buckle and stupid nancy petal-shaped holes in that part of the upper that covered the toes. A pedoscope wasn't needed for those. Through the daft holes you could see if they fitted or not, and in any case they were cheap, the soles made mostly out of some sort of moulded rubber. When I clumped up to the platform for the pedoscope, it felt as though I was wearing the boxes and not the shoes they contained. Far heavier than sandals or even wellies, the proper black, sensible lace-ups made me walk like a circus clown: very deliberately, with bowed legs, like I was learning how to do it all over again.

The wonder – even miracle – of the pedoscope was that at the click of a button on the side and with a very satisfactory buzz, it X-rayed your feet so that parents could check whether or not the sensible shoes fitted properly, and not depend on the unreliable opinion of a sulky child. After shoving my shod feet in a slot at the bottom, and after Ma and the assistant at the Store Footwear Department had had their look and got out of the road, I was allowed to clamp my eye-sockets to the eyepiece (an important added ingredient was that this looked dead like the bit at the bottom of a periscope in a U–Boat where the *Kapitan* looked into it, turned and said, with an evil smile, 'Open ze torpedo doors') and stare at the bones in my feet. I could have done it for hours. Wriggling my toes was exciting, watching the bones move, the joints bend and each foot flex and relax, amazed that they were both mine. It was an everyday wonder, the pedoscope.

'They feel a bit, well, sort of tight, or maybe, loose, Ma.' I had to be prized off the buzzing machine as the queue of five-year-olds built up behind me. Everybody I knew was clumping around the Store Footwear Department in sensible school shoes.

A wooden pencil case with a sliding notched lid and a cargo of an HB, a 2B, a silvery sharpener and a rubber eraser went into the bag from the Hardwear Department and this, said Bina, left plenty of room for a grand leavie-piece. A what? A sandwich to be eaten at 11a.m. when there was fifteen minutes of playtime. Fifteen minutes? Bina promised jam and real butter. But what if I don't like it? Raspberry jam, your favourite. No. What if I don't like the school?

As we lay in bed on the rainy Sunday night, looking out at the half dark of the summer, Bina tried first to encourage me. 'Your Dad was clever at the school. I wasn't, but your Dad got first in the class. He was clever.'

Since I had absolutely no sense of my Dad as a child, and he rarely said anything about when he was young, this notion washed over me. And anyway if he was clever, why did he do exactly the same sort of work as everybody else's Dad, the ones who were second, third, fourth in the class? And why did we all live in the same sort of council house? Clever was clearly nothing much.

Very patiently and with plenty of pauses to check it was all sinking in, Bina began to explain to me the rest of my life. You had to go to the school. It didn't matter much if you didn't like it. You couldn't just stop going because you didn't like it. You had to go. In fact you really weren't supposed to like it. 'I had to go and I didn't.' They learned you things at the school. That was it. You had to be learned to read, write, count and do what you were told. Outside it seemed to rain harder and harder, overflowing the guttering above Bina's bedroom window.

And then when you had finished the school, you had to go to your work. It wasn't exactly the same as the school, but you had to go to your work on the Monday morning and do what you were told. And if you didn't like it, well, that was normal. Most folk didn't like their work. But you had to do it. And that lasted, every Monday morning until, always assuming you were spared, you got the Old Age Pension. And even then there were still socks to darn and kail to be made.

Up to that Sunday night, even on the day when we went to get the smelly schoolbag, none of this had occurred to me. But now, for doing absolutely nothing to anybody at all, ever, I was to be sent to prison, made to join the long grey queue that led to the Post Office and the Old Age Pension, if you were spared. And what was all this about doing what you were told? Who did the telling? And what would happen if you didn't do it? What was worse than school, work and the Old Age Pension?

Inch Road Infants School looked like a prison. Outside its high railings with spiky tops and the tarmacked exercise yard for the grey uniformed children was the World, the place where Cobey, Bindie, Bob, Colin and I had Technicolor adventures and went home for our tea when we were hungry, not when we were let out. Inside were the Misses. Miss MacRae, Miss Elliot, Miss Hood, Miss Brown. And wee Mr MacLennan, the Head-misster. When Bina took me along Inch Road on the Monday morning and in through the big iron gates under a copper beech tree that grew miraculously straight out of the tarmac, she held my hand. We never held hands. I still dislike it. But I can remember clearly Bina holding my hand under the dark branches of the copper beech. We seemed to stand there for a long time.

The Misses were out, directing the milling infants, sorting the bewildered into lines at the foot of the steps leading up into the new building. But after a time Bina took me around the corner to the old part that looked like a bit of a church, and into a room with high windows, too high to see out of.

And then she disappeared. Gone. While I was talking to her. I turned around and Bina had vanished, left me by myself in the big room with thirty other five-year-olds. Before I could make it to the door, wee Mr MacLennan came in with one of the Misses. He said something about the Miss, and then began, 'Children, when you have something to say, hold up your hand and say "Please Miss", and then wait until your teacher points to you.' What? Was this for all the other children? Since I could form the words, I had chattered and talked all day to Bina, and yet here was a little man Ernie Woodhead could probably thump telling me that I could no longer speak. I was to be dumb until someone pointed at me.

Mr MacLennan took off his little gold specs, put them in a case, cracked it shut and left. Miss Brown began to explain that the first thing we would all do was to take our sensible lace-up shoes off and put them neatly under our coat pegs. The pegs had a number and soon we would learn what it was so that we could always put our coat (we didn't have any – it was August) in the same place. One at a time. Girls first. And then we were to take our sandshoes out of our schoolbags. Sorry? Sandshoes? I took out the greaseproof paper package protecting my leavie-piece, and thought briefly about eating it. Then my wooden pencil-case. And then, nothing. No sandshoes. I checked the little pocket stitched on the front of my rigid new schoolbag for a collapsible pair of sandshoes. But nothing. Bina had forgotten them, and I didn't know I had any. Around me all of the other children were producing pair after pair of brilliant white sandshoes, like rabbits out of top hats.

'And then, children,' oh God, there's something else, 'I want you to put them on and line up, girls first, in front of me and I'll show you how to tie your own shoelaces.'

I shuffled in at the back, hoping hard that magic sandshoes would suddenly wrap around my stockinged feet. When I reached the head of the queue, I did the only thing possible and burst into tears.

Having raced along Inch Road and wheeled down to 42 Inchmead Drive, I burst into the kitchenette to find Bina making my dinner. Between gasping sobs, breaking up each word into tear-stained syllables, I breathlessly recounted the tragedies of the morning. I can still feel Bina's hands rhythmically clapping my back as she cuddled me in close, hands on the back of my head, stroking, soothing me quiet. 'There, there. There you are now.' Her pinny smelt of freshly peeled tatties and her cheek of lavender, always lavender.

I needed my sandshoes. You couldn't go to the school without your sandshoes. Where were my sandshoes? I still didn't know how to tie my shoelaces. It didn't matter that like every other child I wore buckled leather sandals in the summertime, I needed to be able to tie my shoelaces, now. I'd be the only one who couldn't. In the whole class. Because I was the only one without sandshoes, the only one who spent the morning in stocking soles. The, only, one.

Bina changed the subject, mashed up some gravy with my tatties and tried to tempt me into eating instead of sobbing. I tried both and sprayed most of my lunch over the oilcloth on the kitchen table. It gradually emerged that there were no sandshoes and even if Bina had been able to walk that far, there was no time to go down the street to the Store Footwear Department to buy a new pair. I thought of the pedoscope and felt momentarily better. After she had scrubbed my mouth and chin with a damp facecloth, Bina held out the straps of my schoolbag and announced that it was nearly time to go back to school. I refused. Not going without my sandshoes. No. Not.

'Help my God! You will have me in Melrose.'

No. And you can't make me. We stared at each other across the kitchen table. It was one of the first in a long line of refusals.

And it was true. Bina couldn't make me. Too old and unsteady to do more than dish out a lick round the ear if I passed nearby, she couldn't chase and certainly not catch me unless I agreed to surrender. And if she hirpled along Inch Road in her slippers to fetch wee Mr MacLennan or Miss Brown, I'd run away for ever before she got back. Hide in a tunnel in the Meadows. And never come back.

Sighing, shaking her head, Bina shuffled through into the living room and lifted her knitting out of her chair by the window before sinking down to look out at all the good children going quietly back to the school after their dinner.

'I'm affronted, just black affronted.'

The quadrant of short grey needles began clacking around the edges of the sock she was knitting out of unravelled wool. Once she was going in a rhythm, Bina could work her way very quickly around a sock, casting on and casting off without ever looking at her hands. I loved to watch her knit, darn and sew because her bent old fingers flew at their jobs, it seemed, with independent mind. Once I remember her knitting while she cried to me over some slight or hurtful remark. Even though her heart was sore and her emotions in turmoil, her amazing swollen and arthritic fingers could knit on regardless. I imagined her making socks of extravagant length as she knitted in one of her snoring sleeps and forgot to cast off.

As Bina's sight began to fail, she never stopped knitting or darning or sewing – the only assistance she needed was in threading her needles or looking for pins as they tinged on to the linoleum. Sometimes she tutted at her fingers, not because they didn't know their work, but when arthritis meant her thimbles no longer fitted properly. There was a wide, open-ended silver thimble designed to slip over the first joint in her thumb to help push a big needle through several thicknesses of cloth. Bina couldn't wear it any more but it would go on the tip of her middle finger when others wouldn't. My fingers, even in my early Fifties, are like my Gran's, bent and beginning to swell at the joints. And instead of her skill and delicacy, I'm becoming clumsy as a result. In Bina's sewing basket lay all sorts of mysterious items: an old green, wooden darning stool, much chipped with use, several sizes of crochet hooks and a ball of yellow beeswax scored in deep lines where thread had been pulled across it to make the sewing easier.

'Wait till your father comes in from his work,' said Bina when the big hand passed 1.30 p.m. and I had not stirred from the pouffe at the fireplace. I was more worried that wee Mr Mac-Lennan would arrive in a police car, a black Morris Oxford screeching to a halt outside 42, bells ringing. Yet another affront. The clock ticked on and Bina knitted without another word.

I grew bored. All my pals had remembered their sandshoes and gone to school, and anyway if I went out in broad daylight someone might report me and the big fat policeman who kicked Ali Boompa's backside would arrive in an instant. And that would be that. Probably had up in court.

'Here, come here,' Bina snapped me out of dreams of incarceration. 'Hold out your hands.'

I moaned. This was the wool-winding position I hated: sitting on the stool opposite her chair with a hank of wool separated by my hands while Bina wound it into a ball.

'You'll get a leathering you know. A right leathering,' she muttered quietly. 'If I tell your Dad, he'll leather you.'

She let that thought sit between us for a while as the ball got bigger and bigger and my arms began to ache.

'Mind you, you look like you're sickening for something.' What? When we finished winding she clamped her hand on my forehead. 'Definitely sickening for something.' I felt fine. 'Probably wouldn't have been fit to go to the school anyway.' What? 'And you didn't take much of your dinner.' I never ate much. Bina smiled at me and put the ball of wound wool into an old floral-print carpet bag. 'Aye, aye, definitely sickening.'

When the back door rattled open at quarter past five to announce my Dad's return from his work, I remembered the promised leathering. But Bina looked at me and put her forefinger to her lips. To keep dirt and dust out of the kitchenette, my Dad peeled off his overalls in the back lobby and hung them on a hook in the coal-hole, and left his boots in the lobby press. Then in his singlet and an old pair of the grey trousers he called flannels, he came through to wash in the kitchenette sink. Soapy water sprayed everywhere as he vigorously washed hands, arms, neck and face. When he was at the sink, my Dad always snorted like a horse as he lathered his face, blowing out his cheeks and grunting. He seemed to hold his breath while washing and exhale noisily when he rinsed. Eyes screwed tight shut, he groped for the towel held out by Gran or my Ma if she was home from work.

On a clear glass Pyrex plate was piled an astonishing mound of food, and it was immediately set down in front of him after the washing and snorting stopped. As a manual worker he needed the calories, but the capacity of his stomach must have been very elastic. Between forking in chips spattered with revolting HP sauce, fried eggs, beans and bread and marg, he enquired about school.

'I'll get the sandshoes down the street tomorrow,' said my Ma. And after an exchange of looks between her and Bina, it was decided that she would go into her work a bit later so that she could take me to the school the following morning.

After a few weeks of saying 'Please, Miss' and doing approximately what I was told, I discovered truancy. At first it seemed absurdly easy. I left 42 with my schoolbag, my leavie-piece and my sandshoes, but instead of going to school, I just kept on going. On the far side of Inch Road stood Dr MacCracken's Wood, a strip of hardwoods and conifers dividing two fields of grazing cows. They were used by Sandy Purves and each morning he drove the black and white Ayrshires along the road to the dairy in Winchester Row where he and his daughter, Agnes, milked them. And then with a stick, a lot of roaring and an old collie, he drove them back to the fields bordering the road. There were so few cars in the early 1950s that no-one saw this quotidian routine as either strange or dangerous.

At the furthest end of Dr MacCracken's Wood stood a tall Scots pine which was screened from view by the large wooded garden behind the doctor's house. Some big boys had nailed up old boards to make a platform between two large branches, and you could sit there out of sight, all day if you wanted. As soon as I climbed the tree, looked carefully around to check that the police had not surrounded the wood, I opened my schoolbag and ate my leavie-piece.

When I did turn up at school I learned to become a prodigious liar. 'My Gran says I'm sickening for something, Miss.' Even when it wasn't really necessary I made up heroic tales of Bina nursing me back from the brink in the space of only a day. 'She said I just wasn't myself.' Who was I then? Stirling Moss? Dan Dare? The Laughing Policeman? But the Misses seemed to accept my stories, no matter how baroque they became. This emboldened me to risk going where people might see me.

I was often drawn down to the Cobby, the wide green riverbank that stretched beside the Tweed from the Duke's Dykes down to Hogarth's Mill. A dangerous, elemental thing, the great river could kill, had taken the lives of children I knew with its invisible currents pulling and holding them down, their pale bodies sometimes found miles downstream, spat out to float on the surface. Broad and deep, the Tweed was able constantly to change, to rumble boulders along its ancient bed, to surge in winter spate over the gardens of Roxburgh Street right up to their back doors and sometimes beyond. Floods brought debris and a wrack of splintered timber, uprooted trees and once a whole barn with its roof above the water floating like an iceberg.

Even when it glided like glass with only the ripples of fish taking a fly, the river held a scary fascination. And on days when I didn't go to the school I liked to play Double Dare on the banks or along at the diving boards. Truth, Dare, Double Dare, Promise or Repeat was a game that only really worked with my pals mooching around the lamppost by the Poorhouse wall, and even better with girls who were always double-dared to take their knickers down. With the river I double-dared myself to step on stones as far out into the current as possible without getting my shorts wet, or to crawl out along the diving board to hang off the end and stare into the brown and shapeless deeps until dizziness persuaded me back to the bank. Once after a spate a huge tree-trunk fetched up on the banks at the Cobby. Broken-off roots projecting in all directions made it look like a large mine bobbing in the North Atlantic, then like a spacecraft just landed. And when I hung my smelly schoolbag on it and climbed up, it became obvious that it was a combine harvester with a dozen gear sticks, controls to raise or lower the cutter and a couple of levers to open the chute from the grain hopper. The sound effects needed to mimic hard work and difficult manoeuvres involved in bringing in the harvest were greatly enhanced by the discovery that the stump would rock from side to side. When it became a tank fighting its way out of a tight corner at El Alamein, or the siege of Berlin, where there were more corners, the impact of near-missing German shells made the rocking more violent. Until. A direct hit. Splash. Into the Tweed over my head.

I couldn't swim, and beside the tottering stump there was a deep pool with a swirling current. Like a flash photograph I saw the stump huge above me, threatening to topple over where I thrashed and gulped the water. And then a pair of hands yanked my arm hard and pulled me spluttering on to the grass. Thank God. It wasn't wee Mr MacLennan, or Miss Brown, or the fat policeman who kicked Ali Boompa's backside. It was a postman.

'Where do you live?'

I squelched up the lane to Roxburgh Street with the postman taking my arm. 'Shouldn't you be at the school?'

When Bina opened the front door of 42 her mouth fell open.

'What in the name of God!' and then I heard her invite 'The Inspector' in. Inspector? The Post Office didn't have inspectors. But he can't have been a real inspector, a police inspector. He didn't kick my backside, take down my name and address in his notebook or have the black and white checked bit on his hat. And he seemed to be very quiet. Policemen always shouted 'Hoi!' If he didn't do any of these things, then perhaps it didn't count.

'This time it'll be a right leathering. The bloody Inspector.

Help my God.' And it was. Belted, sent to bed, no tea. From then on either Bina or my long-suffering sister Barbara took me to the school every morning with my hand held in a vice-like grip. Bina used to stand under the copper beech until the lines of children actually moved in to hang up their coats on the numbered pegs. At least she waved and I waved back.

Having spent many days in Dr MacCracken's Wood or at the Cobby, I had fallen far behind the class and couldn't read or write properly for a long time. And because I was also thought to be both dim and disruptive as well as slow, I found myself in the backward group. Which was grand. With the other outcasts, and the black-haired Romany children shoved into the school for the winter, I made unusable raffia mats (instead of weaving the coloured strands in and out of the warp strings attached to the piece of cardboard, I just wound them round and round – yet more evidence, if it was needed), cut out cork circles for putting a very small teapot on, did a lot of colouring in and tried to keep quiet.

In Miss MacRae's class justice was summary, swift and swingeing. For laughing and pointing when Violet Taylor peed her pants, I was made to stand in the rubbish bin, because I was rubbish. And for swearing and giving her cheek (sadly I've forgotten the details) Miss MacRae locked me in the chalk cupboard for a morning. And when she heard me tipping out the dusty green and pink boxes of chalk on the floor, I was dragged along to wee Mr MacLennan to get the tawse.

The tawse was bad, dead bad, but nothing special. In the 1950s seven- and eight-year-old primary schoolchildren were routinely belted with a thick leather strap split in two at the business end. Watching with pursed satisfaction, the vengeful Miss MacRae folded her arms while wee Mr MacLennan sighed, took off his gold grannie specs, rolled up a sleeve and with little enthusiasm gave me three on each hand.

When he brought a coconut to school, Buff Kyle supplied one of the few educational moments in Miss MacRae's class. Deeply tanned and sporting a remarkable accent, Buff had come back home from Australia and acquired a coconut still in its husk somewhere on his travels. Perhaps the ship had stopped in Africa long enough to let Buff and his pals hire some elephants, go on safari in the jungle, shoot a few lions and tigers, and if they were peckish pick a coconut off a passing palm tree. Everyone had seen small, brown and hairy coconuts glued to their stands at the Shows, but this was a huge, beige-coloured flaky thing almost as big as Ecky Black. On the steps outside Miss MacRae's classroom Buff peeled off the husk, like he knew what he was doing, to reveal a large chocolate brown coconut. With a screwdriver and a hammer one of the janitors knocked out the eyes at the top and poured the pale grey milk into a bowl. Which only Buff and I would drink. And then with the hammer the jannie broke into the brilliant white flesh. Which Buff and I ate.

Miss MacRae was often in touch with God, her rock of ages past, the Father, Son and Holy Ghost. During the rumbling murmur of the Lord's Prayer I could hear Him coming, or His Son, Ghosting around the classroom, watching out for bad behaviour when Miss MacRae had her back turned while she was writing something on the blackboard for the clever sooks at the front to copy out in their brown-paper-covered exercise jotters, cheesy creeps. He could tell even if you were only think-ing about being bad, about how to pick up some fresh dog-shit without touching it and put it in Miss MacRae's desk during playtime. Marie Anderson said that everybody had a guardian angel, but that was OK for her because all the girls were good, even Violet Taylor. She only had a wee problem, it wasn't proper evil badness like Biffo Ford spitting in Mr Johnson's cup of tea while he was out in the playground having a fag. Anyway my guardian angel didn't do much guarding when it came to the Woodheads, in fact the very idea of having one made me feel queasy, uneasy, like somebody reading over your shoulder all the time, somebody breathing on your neck and you couldn't see them, just knew they were there for all eternity. And he'd tell on you as well. Everything, even things you thought about but didn't actually do still counted, were written down in this big white book by God so that when you died and stood in front of Him, He read out all the bad stuff. Then He slammed the book shut, glared over the top of it at you for a minute, and then pulled the lever to open the trapdoor to Hell. Straight down a long black hole and into a bottomless sea of dog-shit. For ever.

All the time I was in the presence of God, Miss MacRae and the Guardian bloody Angels, I concentrated on not dying. And trying not to be as bad as Biffo Ford. I always looked left, looked right, looked left again and then waited until Inch Road was entirely empty of traffic. You were OK so long as you didn't die. That was when they got you, when you were at your most vulnerable, when you were dead. Immortality was certainly preferable to swimming with Biffo in limitless oceans of snot, sick and dog-shit, but who wanted to go to Heaven and be with all the cheesy, good people who spent all their time not doing anything bad or interesting.

Bina used to spread her bets, take out lots of celestial insurance policies. Until her corns made slippers a constant necessity, my Gran put on her hat every Sunday morning and went at least once to all the churches in Kelso, except the catholics of course. Perhaps she was auditioning. Finally settling on the biggest one with the tallest spire (it was also the nearest to 42), she also acquired a church elder. Most weeks Mr Calton used to come visiting at Inchmead Drive and Bina made him tea with a buttered scone and jam. Not Stork, real butter.

A retired banker, Mr Calton was tall, gaunt, precise and a very tidy eater. Each time he took a bite of Bina's scone, he picked up the plate and held it under his bony chin. Crumbs worried Mr Calton. So that none fell and disappeared into the deep pile of his jaggy Harris tweed suit, he gently shook the scone before lifting it to his mouth, and his bite was always a tiny mouse nibble with lots of lip movement to make absolutely sure everything was gobbled in and nothing fell. There were often long silences in the living room while Mr Calton drank his tea, pinkie extended, spoon placed and replaced to the left of the saucer, cup handle to the right, and Bina knitted her brows in silent admonition if I fidgeted too much or sighed too audibly. Once Mr Calton arrived in a new blue suit which he carefully arranged before sitting down. Muttering in the back kitchen after he had gone, Bina disapproved, 'Never get the wear out of it, man of his years.'

One afternoon, halfway through a long silence, my Gran told her church elder a lie. A black lie.

'He's looking for a nice hobby,' she said, nodding towards me, sitting minding my own business on the pouffe by the fireplace. What!? What's a bloody hobby when it's at home? What was she on about?

'Is that a fact?' replied Mr Calton, checking his lap for stray crumbs and brushing away the ones that were only visible through a microscope. No it isn't! This was quickly developing into one of those conversations when any word from me would have greeted by a glare, even though they were talking about me.

'I have an extensive collection of stamps,' announced the old man after a lengthy pause. And that was it. The next week I was scrubbed, checked for crumbs, given a row and sent round to Mr Calton's house to begin my new hobby. It didn't apparently matter that I didn't have any stamps myself and couldn't think why I should want any. I never wrote letters, or anything else.

Poynder Place was posh. It still is. And unlike everybody in Inchmead Drive, Mr Calton used the front door and Bina told me that I was to ring the bell and wait. But it turned out to be a bell-pull and it baffled me. After pressing it a dozen times, twiddling it, searching the surface of the door for a bell that worked or a letterbox knocker I could rattle, I decided that he wasn't in. And at the very moment I turned away he opened the front door. Behind it was darkness.

A heavy curtain fell as I squeezed past into the vestibule, and on the other side of a half-glazed door there seemed to be no light at all in the hall except a window about a hundred yards away at the bottom of a short staircase. In the parlour the brown-paper blinds were drawn against the afternoon sun and as I was ushered around the screen by the door, I hit my knee on a small set of library steps. To suit the decor of his shadowy house Mr Calton wore brown and looked pale grey in the dim light.

We sat down at the fireplace and he gave me a cigar box full of stamps. 'They're all doubles and none of them very old. Enough for a good start.'

Then he showed me his stamp albums. Leather-bound with index tabs sticking out of the pages, they were organised by continent and country, and as he slowly leafed through, I thought they were wonderful. Richly coloured, intricately detailed, like miniature banknotes, the stamps told stories. Mr Calton pointed out that most carried the name of their country of origin, often ones I had never heard of or didn't recognise. Suomi was Finland, Sverige was Sweden and Norsk was Norway. Many carried beautiful portraits of leaders, presidents or monarchs. Those of Queen Juliana of the Netherlands seemed so perfect as to be tiny photographs. And when we leafed over to Germany there were dozens of stamps showing the head of Adolf Hitler.

After the last stamp from Swaziland had been looked at, Mr Calton gave me a small packet of clear gummed transfers. They were to be folded over and while one side was carefully stuck to the back of the stamp, the other was stuck to the page of the album. Fiddly but essential. On no account should I ever stick a stamp straight on to the page. That made it valueless and impossible to move if you wanted to swap it. And then, just as I thought I should be going home, Mr Calton took a small folder out of his bureau and untied the cloth tapes around it. 'These,' he lifted the leaves of the folder to reveal another one, this time made out of gossamer tissue, 'are rare, and I believe, valuable.' One looked as if it had been written rather than printed while some of the others had Queen Victoria's head on them.

For my birthday Bina did an unusual thing, she bought me

a present. It was Stanley Gibbons' *First Stamp Album* and I passed
a wonderful rainy afternoon licking all the stamps Mr Calton
had given me and sticking them straight on to the pages. But it
worked, it did become a serious hobby for a while and when
I sat down to look through my album, it felt like there were
worlds out there in Suomi or Sverige or Norsk, maybe not
Deustchland, or Hellas or Magyar or Espana, whole worlds
beyond Inchmead Drive.

Inch Road Infants School was bursting at the seams with post-
war baby boom children. At between thirty and forty, classes
were large and accommodation inadequate. In the hall of the
Church of Scotland's St John's Edenside, Mrs Boles taught us a
great deal about catholicism. Perhaps the hovering shade of John
Knox moved her to explain regularly that statues of the Virgin
Mary were not worshipped like idols, that confession and abso-
lution were cleansing acts, and that the Pope would always bless
poor sinners, although possibly drawing the line at Protestants.
This was bewildering, but nothing like as strange as the Friday
afternoon book.

Mrs Boles was fond of the Famous Five, and for the last hour
of the week she read aloud the tales of Julian, Dick, Anne,
George and their dog Timmy. Entirely foreign, involving elab-
orate sequences turning on the exercise of good manners, a great
deal of business about picnics and something called 'pop', and all
done in a sunlit, summery, cottagey countryside, the Famous
Five exerted a profound influence. Mrs Boles' readings from
Enid Blyton introduced me to the deeply reassuring mythic
world of the English middle classes – as an observer from another
planet. So long as honesty, politeness, an understanding of complicated hierarchies and careful cycling informed behaviour, well
then, everything would be perfectly all right, wouldn't it.

Although much of it was baffling, I longed to convert the
stories into the Famous Six, pedalling hard up the steep country

lane with high hedges on either side and freewheeling down home to tea with Mother or Uncle Somebody-or-Other, breathlessly recounting completely safe adventures where something almost happened, but at the last minute didn't, all being redeemed by honesty, politeness and a knowledge of the Highway Code. Perhaps what attracted me to upright Julian, his wholesome chums and their ordered world was the fact that I was a compulsive liar, a constant swearer, did not own a bicycle and, according to Miss MacRae, was rubbish.

Pressure of numbers, teacher-knows-best traditions and an inherited highhandedness persuaded Inch Road Infants to tell parents as little as possible about the education of their children. Annual report cards and tear-stained reports back after a belting or a humiliation were generally the only conduits of information. Parents very rarely met or contacted their children's teachers directly. And when they were summoned to school, it was usually to hear bad news. Until Mrs Boles complained that I repeatedly contradicted her (by some forgotten means – perhaps from Mr Calton's stamps – I had discovered that The Hague was the political capital of Holland while Mrs Boles insisted the real capital was Amsterdam, and everyone knew that on the coloured map unrolled on the wall there could be only one capital to each country) my parents had little idea that I was being taught as a backward child. Reactions at 42 were very different. My Ma was furious and determined to change the situation. After all, was not my older sister Barbara clever at the school and my younger sister Marjie getting on well? Why should I be different? It was the school that was wrong. When she heard the news Bina shook her head and stared out of the window, wondering if it was her fault that I was as stupid as her. And my Dad? It turned out he was ready to give up on me and agree with Miss MacRae and Mrs Boles. Teachers knew best. Always had.

At eight or nine I was too big to carry on sleeping with Bina. My parents moved out of the front bedroom and let me have their double bed. This forced them to buy a big convertible sofa called a 'studio' settee from the Store Furnishings and Upholstery Department. Every night in life, no matter how dog-tired they were, they had to make it up into a bed. The metal frame of the red studio settee was unfolded flat, the cushions laid out, sheets and blankets tucked under, pillows thrown down and a quilt set on top. My Ma must have thought often of the spacious accommodation in The Dispensary.

Upstairs Bina had one bedroom where we both used to sleep, Barbara and Marjie were in another and I had the last one. Because the front bedroom over looked the street, I could often hear the arrival and departure of snatches of conversation as people walked past on the pavement below. Most Saturday nights my Dad went down the street to the Red Lion or the Black Swan for a few pints of beer while my Ma stayed at home. Sometimes he brought her back a Schweppes bottle with some gin or whisky and lemonade in it. If I was awake after ten o'clock, I could hear his distinctive voice as he walked back along the pavement with a neighbour and occasionally they would stop at the gate and talk for a while. On calm nights their voices were easily made out, not competing with traffic or anything else, and in my mind I can hear the deep, bass tones crystal clearly. One night, around the time when news of my educational shortcomings had leaked out of the prison that was Inch Road Infants, I heard my Dad come to a stop at the gate.

'Can't bloody well understand it. Stupid. Just seems to be stupid, empty. Nothing there but trouble. And cheeky, argues with the teachers. Just stupid, stupid.'

There was more, a lot more, but after the sinking realisation that my own Dad was talking about me, like that, I stopped taking it in. I kept thinking that he was talking to someone outside our family about me, saying that I was useless, stupid, empty. I wished I had got up out of my bed, shoved up the window and shouted for him to stop, or found it wasn't him, or he didn't really mean it, or he was drunk. But I just lay in the big double bed where he used to sleep and listened to him betray me. Why? Bina loved me. My Ma loved me and would fight for me. Why did my Dad think I was useless? Why was I nothing to him? Just because the teachers didn't like me.

This was the first but no means the last time I heard him talk about me below my window on a Saturday night. Over several years, into my teens, he discussed my inadequacies several times with other people. I remember once finding myself on the wrong end of a thumping at schoolboy rugby and my Dad remarking to a neighbour that it was only to be expected because I was just 'a shit, a shit in a bottle. No heart'. Other, worse things I have blanked out over the years, perhaps in an unconscious effort to forgive him.

That Saturday night long ago something in me was severed. I was already scared of my Dad's rages and his fists, but then most of my pals felt the same way about their fathers. There was nothing untoward in regular leatherings from your Dad – in those days it was expected. But after I heard him disparage and betray me, I could never bring myself to trust him again, and as I grew older I paid less and less attention to his advice or his splenetic judgements. In fact I generally tried to do the opposite of what he wanted, using refusals for small revenges. But what he represented mattered to me, mattered desperately.

I wanted to have a Dad who supported me, was always on my side no matter what or who, and who sometimes said 'Well done, son'. All my life he never said that. Never. Even when something appeared to go well or succeed in however small a way, he always managed to find a problem with it, the one thing that wasn't quite right, and might even spell doom, or a come-uppance of some dastardly sort. I couldn't know it then, when I was a truanting, unco-operative primary schoolboy, but these miserable attitudes were ultimately his loss, not mine.

FOUR

Show Business

'WE'RE OFF TO see the Wizard, the Wonderful Wizard of Oz. Tarum Tee Ta, Tarum Tee Ta, Tarum Tee Tum, Tee Tum, Tee Tum.' We both were, my big sister and me, down to the Roxy's Saturday matinee to see the Wizard, the Wonderful Wizard of Oz. All the way along Forestfield Barbara skipped and sang the chorus over and over, dragging me behind in the usual vice-like grip. 'Shut up your moaning! You'll like it. I did.'

There was a queue that looked very like the lines on a Monday morning outside Inch Road Infants School. And when we finally got inside the foyer, the world changed and the bewildering, hypnotic, nauseating kaleidoscope of Technicolor began to fill my widening eye. Lurid purples, oranges and yellows on the walls, and for my immediate visit to the toilet (leaving Barbara huffing as the queue behind us got ahead of us) a dark brown corridor down steps to eyewatering ammonia. Lining the walls were pictures of people with pancake and scarlet complexions: Jeff Chandler had yellow hair, Lucille Ball an unlikely vermilion bosom and adhesive lips, Victor Mature's lips were bigger and his bosom only a little smaller, Ava Gardner looked like Victor Mature's big sister, Jayne Mansfield had the hugest bosom, white teeth and white hair while William Holden scowled in a chocolate suit, smoking a cigarette. It was dizzying, blinkingly disorienting, like living inside a cartoon. And it scared me.

I didn't know it was her yet, but the Wicked Witch of the West ushered us and a dozen others to our row of seats. Lank black hair, a hooked nose balancing tiny National Health specs and a searching torch-beam spotlighting miscreants, missile-throwers and the farting competition in the front row, Auld Jean was the incarnation of Terror, ruling the Roxy with the flick of a switch. And it was rumoured that she was somebody's mother. Perhaps Zeke Lillie's?

The red curtains trundled apart, music wound up to speed, the numbers flickered, counting down, and to an ecstatic cheer far beyond even Auld Jean's control, Woody Woodpecker burst through the screen. 'Ha, Ha, Ha, HA-Ha!' There was a big boy sitting in front of me and I hid behind him until I was sure that a giant Woody wouldn't come waddling up the aisle. Then a short film about bears in Your Semmit National Park, or some-where. The commentary made them sound like furry versions of The Broons', or somebody, with Momma and Poppa goin' fishin' with the kids. 'Now little 'un, this is how you do it. Pay attention, son,' said Poppa as he bit the head off a wriggling salmon. 'And as the sun sets on the Rocky Mountains at the end of another day, Momma takes the kids back to the den while Poppa goes off in search of supper' – and to rip the throat out of another terrified animal.

After Pathé and Pearl & Dean, Barbara went to get me a tub of rock-hard ice-cream with a miniature wooden shovel, which I immediately dropped amongst the sticky debris under the seats. Even scrabbling on the floor after my shovel I could see Auld Jean's torch flash and pan around the cinema like searchlights in the Blitz and after a chorus of shushing and an isolated fart from the front row, I heard the curtains trundle open again, and hushed comments that the big picture was starting. No sign of the wooden shovel.

Back on my seat to look at the vast screen and a picture of a better-looking woman holding a different sort of torch from Auld Jean's. I bit the tub but got nothing more than a tiny chip. Breathing on it didn't work, so back down on the floor for another grope amongst the rubbish. I found a second-hand lolly stick and looked out from behind the big boy's seat. All I could see was a wee girl with the same pancake and scarlet complexion as Lucille Ball, and a dog. No sign of the Wizard, just a landscape that complemented the interior decor of the Roxy. Huge Cinemascope images in sickeningly lush colours followed; vile egg-yolk yellow counterpointed with lurid rhubarb-leaf green. And I had less idea than Toto what was going on.

The soundtrack bounced along as Dorothy wended her weird way through wherever she was, cheerfully chatting to whatever bizarre apparition presented itself out of the lurid shrubbery. The plot being lost on me, the gigantic images began to impress themselves very powerfully, and as in a bad dream in Bina's bed the cinema seemed to tilt slightly to one side, making me feel smaller and smaller, overwhelmed by purple flowers, yellow bricks and fluorescent Munchkins. And we hadn't even seen the Wizard yet. The Technicolor world spun and flashed over the big boy's shoulder and I took respites in the comforting darkness behind his seat.

But when Dorothy met the Tin Man, I was seized with sudden panic. Dropping my ignored and melted ice-cream I ran up the aisle, pushed past Auld Jean through the orange double doors, fled between Victor Mature and Ava Gardner and burst out into the normal, stable, safe sunshine of the Roxy car park. Mrs Hall was coming out of Pratt the Grocer's opposite and she waved at me. I waved back, gasping and wailing with relief. And then I wailed louder, because my big sister belted me.

'Stop it! Stop it!'

She was furious at being dragged away from the bit where the Cowardly Lion, the Tin Man, Dorothy and Toto dance about on the Yellow Brick Road. I wanted to vomit, and with ice-cream all over my shorts, it looked as though I had.

'You rotten little bugger!'

Before anyone had the money for bicycles, buses or cars, my Ma and her sister, Auntie Isa, went for walks. On fine spring evenings when the chill was at last off the winter and the ground had come alive with snowdrops, daffodils, crocuses and primroses, I was dragged out with Barbara, Marjie and the pram for when she got tired, and my cousins Davina and Isbel. They were long walks, often returning home when it was more than gloaming. When they were young Ma and her sisters had thought nothing of walking five or ten miles to dances at one of the village halls around Hawick. They just did it as though the time and effort it took were natural parts of life, not a waste or a problem but something routinely done and enjoyed. Even into middle age and with children trailing behind the habit died hard though the need had long gone. It extended their day beyond work, cooking and housework, let some light into their circumscribed lives. Auntie Isa was older than my Ma and never lost her delight, punctuated by the magical laughing smile all those sisters had, in telling tales of daftness and embarrassments in their upbringing at Allars Crescent, a street of tenements behind the west end of Hawick High Street.

'Well washed' was my Ma's description of the countryside after the winter, after the first green had covered the fields. At the far end of Kelso Bridge, beyond what came to be called Bridgend Park, there stood a replica of a Roman triumphal arch with rusty iron gates set unsteadily under it. On the other side an overgrown driveway led nowhere. Once in a day there had been a grand house at the end of it, but when the Douglas family died out, it was dynamited flat. But in a heyday not so long before, the estate entrance had been made far more glorious than the out-of-place arch because gardeners had planted thousands of snowdrops and daffodils in the steep bank above it. When my Ma and Auntie Isa took us walking there, the hopeful whites and sumptuous yellows covered the ground with hundreds of thousands of flowers that remembered the work of all those men and gave the place its name, Springwood. We never picked any snowdrops or daffodils for reasons now forgotten – not because of anxieties about theft (who could object?) but, I suspect, out of unspoken reverence for the majesty, exuberance and abundance of the thing. Springtime also took us further along the Teviot Road to Daniel's Den. On a vertiginous river-cliff above the Tweed many clumps of primroses grew, and these my Ma did pick, for she loved the shape of the flower. All of the girls walked back through the evening into the town with one in each lapel.

Cobey could speak like a cowboy. When it was his birthday he invited Bindie, Bob, Colin and me to come round to his back door for a shindig. His Ma had some tattie scones and we could have, well, a shindig. They had them all the time in Westerns and that was both reason and explanation enough.

At Cobey's insistence we checked our guns at the back door of his saloon and solemnly handed over all our caps. He didn't want no trouble. My Winchester Rifle used singles and I laid down their small, green, circular cardboard container while Bindie's Colt 45 had rolls of caps wound inside. The atmosphere was edgy, each gunfighter quiet and watchful as he munched a tattie scone.

'OK fellers,' drawled Cobey, 'let's play a little poker.' None of us knew what poker was, but this was Cobey's shindig. There followed an awkward pause which made it clear that he didn't know either.

'OK, let's saddle up and high-tail it outa here.' Buckling on our gunbelts, we smacked our own backsides with the long reins and cantered round to the front garden and across the path to look at some Apache horses.

Mounted on a thick hedge of elder and beech, we could see at least one standing some distance from our wagon train. Accra spooked when Bindie fired off some caps and it trotted over to be next to Paddy, Chief Sitting Bull's favourite pony. Like timid bullfighters we sometimes dropped down off the hedge and into the field, and if either horse looked up from its grazing we immediately sprinted back to safety. In a fit of stunning bravado Dave MacKay once crept up through the grass, like an Apache, behind Accra and pulled his tail. He was rewarded with a sickening kick in the face and Bina warned me never to go near the horses again. And anyway they belonged to Matt Ballantyne and not bloody Geronimo.

Horses on screen were safer and Cobey persuaded me to go to the Roxy to see the Westerns and the cowboys he idolised. Having been assured that the Tin Man was not playing the Sheriff of Tombstone, I agreed to the first of many sixpenny matinees, and a thousand wagon trains were happily pursued by a million whooping Apaches. On the way back up to Inchmead Drive Cobey and I often galloped ahead to lay an ambush for Bindie, Bob and Colin. The narrow canyon of Forestfield was dangerous and if the English Kirk minister was not washing his car on a Saturday afternoon, we climbed up behind his redbrick gateposts with our rifles cocked and caps stuck on with spit. In the distance, far across the prairie, a dust cloud rose on Edenside Road and hoofbeats drummed, mixed with war cries, 'AooA, AooA, AooA.' And if the Woodheads had been to the Roxy and were pursuing the Apaches, the hoofbeats got faster, and Cobey and I ducked down out of sight behind the minister's gatepost.

Forestfield's villas housed much of Kelso's small middle class, but not all of those who had aspirations. The nearby rows of council houses in Inch Road and Inchmead Drive looked the same; one after the other with grey harling, grey slates and black front doors. While back gardens produced similarly prosaic quantities of vegetables, the front offered variety, the opportunity to be different. Conventional formats laid out a square or rectangular green and bordered it with sober colour schemes of bedding plants. Sometimes a round bed was cut into the middle of the green or a rockery set on a sloping end. Mr and Mrs Hawkins had more to show than most since they were on a corner site and some of their back garden was at the front. Tidy, hoed rows of vegetables were segregated by a box hedge from the formalities of the alyssums, asters and primulas. Others had even more colourful summer shows of flowers that lit the grey council estate, but no-one had what the Hawkinses had. No-one.

Miss Stella Ballantyne came to their house. I saw her myself. It was definitely her, the most beautiful woman in the world, not counting the ones in the Roxy, who didn't count on account of not being real, like her. Big boys from the High School, where she was a teacher, stared at Miss Ballantyne when she walked along Inch Road to visit the Hawkinses. But she didn't care. Things like that didn't matter if you were as beautiful as Stella Ballantyne. Once when I was sitting on a wagon in the hedge by the horsefield, she passed quite close to me, and although I tried, I couldn't help looking at her either.

Elegant. That was it. Seeming to walk quite slowly, Miss Ballantyne executed each step as if it were part of a dance playing inside her head. Dark hair, cut short like but better than Jeanne Moreau, and specs with little wings on the top corner of each frame, she had what the French called gamine looks and the Scots just stared at. I imagined that, like in films, the effect of Miss Ballantyne taking off her winged specs would be devastating, making the big boys from the High School sit down or grasp at a nearby rail or wall, and making me fall out of the hedge.

Brian Hawkins knew about these things. He got to get married to Stella Ballantyne, but only because he was very good-looking and very pleasant to everybody. Nobody liked him of course, except her. And Mr and Mrs Hawkins.

Each summer there was an excuse to hang around outside their house. Barrie and Peter came to stay with Nana Hawkins for their holidays, a break from somewhere far away in the west like Coatbridge or Kilmarnock, Kilwinning or Kilbarchan. Like a miniature man with V-necked pullovers and a parting in his thick hair, Barrie commanded an assurance and posh vocabulary far beyond anything Bindie, Cobey, Bob, Colin or I could muster between the five of us. And he was hard as well. Once when Peeny MacLeod challenged him to a fight in Shedden Park, Barrie stunned the circling crowd by adopting a Queens-berry Rules position, fists up and feet apart. Peeny just looked at him, mouth agape. And when he finally lunged at Barrie, a sidestep sent him grasping at the air. 'Oh, I see. Scrag fighting is it?' observed the Wee Man From the Wilder West, somewhat distantly, as he jumped on Peeny's back and shoved his head into the grass. Watching unconcerned, with his arms folded, the younger brother, Pete, had seen it all before.

Barrie also knew all about swings. In Shedden Park there was a green-painted set hung on long chains from a tall tubular frame, and nearby a roundabout and a seesaw. What Barrie understood was etiquette. Everyone wanted to play on the swings, the roundabout and the seesaw, but what he knew was how to organise demand into an orderly sequence of what was fair. If you wanted to go on the swings then you boosted for the person in front. Although for how long this went on was less clear – perhaps it was until they were swinging as high as they wanted, or perhaps as high as you could get them. With Cobey that wasn't very high, with Colin Purves it could be 360 degrees. Barrie also showed us how to swing while standing on the seat, how to boost yourself by pushing with your feet and flexing your legs.

On the seesaw he stood astride the fulcrum, shifting his weight to even up the disparity between Cobey and everybody else, and showing us how to use our legs to prevent a bum-banging landing. And on the roundabout Barrie was the lord of the turning world. While we spun the roundabout, he stood in the middle, hands on hips, defying dizziness, even smiling at those below. We were enthralled, his new friends, and we trailed behind Barrie on the road back up to Inchmead Drive.

'I'll ask my Nana if we can all watch *Boots and Saddles*.' Looks of disbelief were exchanged. Everyone knew that in addition to the visits of Stella Ballantyne, the Hawkinses enjoyed another unique distinction. They had a television. No-one had ever seen it except them and the only sound evidence of its actual existence, its presence in their living room, was the time when Bob Swan's men came round to fix a huge aerial on to their chimney. It looked like a garden grape for a giant's vegetable patch. Barrie had the television at home in Kilbirnie or Paisley and, in his opinion, the finest programme was definitely *Boots and Saddles*. We nodded. But when Nana Hawkins saw her summer visitors having the front gate held open for them by us, she had to think quickly. My sister Marjie knew her as a formidable and resourceful woman. Down the street one Saturday morning, Mrs Hawkins had said briskly, 'Good morning Barbara.' 'But I'm Marjorie.' 'Are you sure?'

Her instant solution to the invasion of the unwashed served all interests. Barrie and Peter removed their sandals at the door and were ushered on to the settee in the living room. Nana then directed me, Cobey, Bindie, Bob and Colin on to the gravel path outside the living room window. Barrie waved from inside. My friends looked in puzzlement at each other. I was looking along Inch Road to see if Stella Ballantyne was coming. In the dark recesses of the interior stood a large sideboard with a vase of flowers on top. These were removed and two doors clipped open to reveal a screen the size of a small window pane. Mr Hawkins twiddled the knobs under it and waited for the television, for this was it, supplied by Robert Swan, to warm up.

After some discussion with her husband, Mrs Hawkins opened the living room window so that we could all hear as well as watch and told Cobey not to lean on the paintwork or poke his rifle into the room. Meanwhile diagonal black-and-white bars appeared on the tiny screen. Was it broken? Barrie turned around and smiled at us. With some adjustments to the horizontal hold, a grey picture finally appeared. It was a posh woman in a dress sitting next to some flowers. You could tell that she thought she was something, but the truth is that she was nothing like as good-looking as Miss Ballantyne and certainly didn't have the complexion of Ava Gardner, or Victor Mature.

'Now children.' Perhaps it was the Queen. 'Are you sitting comfortably? Now it's time for another exciting story from the Wild West.' Cobey stifled a cheer. This was not the Roxy but something happening in a living room three doors away from his. Barrie turned round again and looked at us. He had delivered, just like he said he would. *Boots and Saddles*. On TV. The bugler sounded the US Cavalry order to mount up. The officer with the tremendous gloves and the crossed sabres on his hat swivelled round in his saddle to nod to his sergeant. He raised his hand and shouted 'Ho, wOoo', and the column moved out of the fort. The Apaches in the mountains exchanged evil looks, and we knew it would be tough. But this was the US Cavalry.

Seven-week summer holidays were long enough to forget that school loomed at their distant end. Most mornings Cobey, Bindie, Bob, Colin and I trooped hopefully round to ask Mrs Hawkins if Barrie and Peter could come out to play.

'They're still having their breakfast.'

The day couldn't start without our shiny new pals and sometimes we had to stand and wait so long that I stamped on a primula in protest. Or we sat in the hedge by the horsefield for a while playing a desultory game of Apaches and wagon trains, wondering what they could be having for their breakfast that couldn't be bolted in less than a minute. Cobey had his in his pocket.

Barrie had a plan, and it almost always involved football. In an age before plastic, he owned the real thing, a leather ball made out of long sewn-together strips containing a pink bladder held in by thick laces. If you headed the ball on the laces, they left a mark that could last for days. None of us were much good at football, but that was OK because Barrie and Peter came from Cumbernauld or Cambuslang in the west of Scotland where they played it all the time. And they were easily good enough for the rest of us. But the long grass in the empty horsefield was a problem for touch-players like Barrie. When it came up to your knees a long pass might get lost for a few minutes and dribbling often involved simultaneous scything. Getting the ball to move at all could be a tremendous effort and attempted hacks out of the really long stuff prompted a lot of swearing. Except from Barrie. He was an enigma. He never swore ever, but at the same time he was really hard.

How did that work? Every other person who was definitely hard swore all the fucking, bastarding, fucking time, you fucking bastard. Fuck. Really loud. Mind you I tended to swear at every fucking opporfuckingtunity, bastard, just for the sheer pleasure of unihibited profuckingfanity. Fuck. But unless I lost my temper, saw the red mist and went into a complete raj, I wasn't considered particularly hard. Peeny MacLeod did burst into tears before we fought in the playground at Inch Road Infants, but that was thought to be a technical victory, not solid evidence of sustained hardness. Ernie Woodhead, on the other hand, was seriously hard, had a tremendous sneer as well, and when it was combined with a few contemptuously spat swearwords, it diminished trembling opponents before a blow was struck. And these effects were enhanced even more by Brylcreem and a heroic saunter of such menace that when Cobey was unexpectedly confronted by Ernie, he looked like Corky the Cat when he got his tail plugged into the mains. Unfortunately, Ernie and Barrie never squared up to each other, like Gary Cooper and the other guy in *High Noon*. Probably because Ernie was just as scared of Nana Hawkins as we were.

After four hours of football we went down the town to the Knowes to watch the Shows being set up. Dodgems, shooting stalls with bent rifles, chairoplanes, candy-floss-making machines, coconut stalls, hoopla, the Waltzer, and most of all, the smell, the unique, narcotic smell of show business. Spun sugar, hot dogs and onions, diesel and oil from the gearings of the Dodgems and the Waltzer, cheap scent, danger, deceit and an unwholesome transience floated into the clear summer air above the town.

And when the Shows opened for each night of Civic Week, the smell of show business was driven by the insistent blare of pop music over the rooftops. Elvis the Pelvis, Billy Fury, Little Richard, Chuck Crazylegs Berry and Adam Faith all seemed to sing louder as the week went on, drowning out the Scottish Home Service, Uncle Mac's Family Favourites and Gardeners' Hour.

The unapologetic, paint-chipped tackiness of the shows was mesmeric – even though its palpable fakery was obvious, even to me. The men, boys and blowsy ladies behind the painted boards of the darts and cards stalls looked blankly at their excited customers, handing out rubber rings, wooden balls and small feathered darts for the bent air rifles. On the Dodgems Brylcreemed boys careened nonchalantly around on the back of the snub-nosed little cars holding on to the metal rods that sparked against the mesh above the polished steel surface. They looked bored, expressionless, just another week in another town, who cares where. Perhaps for those who only saw the Shows once in a blue moon, a gossamer moment in another world beyond the everyday could be glimpsed over the rainbow colours of the Waltzer.

Barrie, Peter, Cobey, Colin, Bob, Bindie and I sat on the Abbey School playground wall to watch the Shows being built. Garishly painted boards with faded copperplate signs announcing each attraction surrounded by fake gilt filigree were unloaded from lorries and trailers and assembled with metronomic efficiency. And in an afternoon a miniature metropolis of fun took shape. Big attractions were framed by smaller stalls supplying a sense of enclosure, a perimeter separating the world of worthless prizes, cheap thrills and candy-floss, from the grey world of going home to bed.

'What time is it?'

'Dunno.'

'Nana said tea was at 5 p.m. and that Peter and I shouldn't be late.'

We slipped off the wall and wandered around the backs of the stalls, feeling like Lord Snooty and His Pals. Except that Cobey, Bob, Colin, Bindie and me looked more like the Bash Street Kids, hands in our pockets, scuffing along the pavement, occasionally squabbling, mooching our way back up to Inchmead Drive with no idea what time it was. Not even what day it was. And Barrie didn't have a watch.

Bindie had an idea though. Plums. In the hushed tones of a growing conspiracy he told us that in the walled garden of a big house over by the riverside, near Hogarth's Mill, there were plum and pear trees that grew up the inside of the walls. Honest. All you had to do was climb the wall and lean over the top to pick some. You didn't have to go in, so how could you get caught? It was probably even legal, like, everybody's, sort of, property, you know. And that. Barrie and Peter hesitated, somewhere between doing the right thing (What would Nana say if we got caught?) and not appearing to be lily-livered, a yella streak right down the middle of their backs, pardner. By the time we got to Oven Wynd, a lane leading down to the Tweed and the targeted garden, Barrie and Peter had joined the Bash Street Kids, while the ghost of Lord Snooty went back up the road to Nana's for his tea at 5 p.m. sharp.

However, Bindie's plan was not perfect. In fact it had a substantial flaw. No ladder. The walls protecting the plum and pear garden were very high and smooth-sided. At the foot of Oven Wynd an unmetalled track went right down to a channel of the Tweed which ran between the bank and a small river island called an anna. Downstream from the great medieval weir built diagonally across the flow, several islands had formed in the middle of the river. And in summer their vegetation was lush, dense and crawling with large, well-fed rats. The weir had originally been thrown across to direct the current to the wheels of Kelso Abbey's ancient mill and although its direct descendant, Hogarth's Mill, no longer needed water power, it did process and store huge quantities of grain and flour. Rats had colonised the river islands in very large numbers, and from them mounted daily raids on the sacks and grain hoppers inside the mill. Once I saw the backside and long orange tail of a rat the size of a small dog as it slid between the weeds into the river. And they were fearsome when cornered, always fighting back whatever the odds. Few people ventured on to the islands without a stout stick and a wary eye for movement in the tangle of elder, reeds and hogweed.

At the foot of Mill Wynd a row of stepping stones ran across the river channel and Bindie hopped out on it to see if the river wall of the plum garden was any easier. It was, but the water below it might be too deep. And anyway . . .

'Hoi!! You! What do you think you're doing!'

A man stood at the top of the lane silhouetted against the light. Huge, with a sack in his hand, he immediately started down the slope towards us.

With no other possible escape, we all slipped and splashed across the stepping stones on to the Island of the Giant Rats and disappeared into the watery jungle. Barrie and Peter were not happy, and everyone else looked nervously around their sandalled feet, wondering if a kick in the backside from the man with the sack would have been preferable to an attack by the Killer Rats.

'What's he doing?' whispered Cobey.

Through the lush stalks and branches we saw the man walk out on the stepping stones and then hurl the sack into the middle of the channel. A cursory glare across at the island made us all duck down, and then he was gone.

'Look,' said Cobey, 'It's wriggling. The sack's moving.'

And it was. Not completely submerged, the tied neck was definitely moving about. All thoughts of plums and pears departed, Bindie and Colin waded into the water and gingerly lifted up the dripping sack. It could be full of particularly dangerous and vicious rats from Hogarth's Mill. When we set it down on the bank, Cobey summoned up all his gumption, untied the string and we all leaped backwards. After more wriggling a very bedraggled kitten crawled out and shook itself. Then two more appeared. Inside the sack we found the drowned corpses of another three. We picked up the tiny creatures and tried to dry them with a hankie.

'They'll want warm milk,' said Bob, 'when we get them back.' Back where?

We took the kittens, rolled up in our front shirt-tails, up the road home. I knew Bina much preferred cats to budgies, but I was sure I wouldn't be allowed to keep one. Cobey and Colin decided that we could build a cat-den in the horsefield hedge and give them some milk every morning, taking it in turns to nick it off the neighbours' doorsteps. What actually happened to the half-drowned survivors has vanished from memory. But what remains is the depth of Barrie and Peter's dumb amazement. For once we surprised and impressed them, for this sort of thing almost never happened in Gourock or Greenock.

Cops were the same though. They aways knew where you were going to be, were ruthless in extracting confessions, and if you said fuck off to a cop, the world fell on your head. One summer, it did. Stealing apples had nothing to with apples. Mostly they were unripe, hard as turnips. What really mattered was the degree of difficulty, the amount of cheek involved and the ability to get away with it, just. But none of these tests applied to the mass arrest at the top of the Bullet Loan in July 1959.

Cobey, Colin, Bindie, Bob and I were in Bridgend Park looking at strange fruit. Around the perimeter of the public park (no high walls, no houses overlooking and no-one watching, no private ownership, no problem, hardly worth it) stood several small trees with something like large cherries growing on them. Bright red and possibly ripe, they dangled just out of our reach. So Bob decided to climb one of the small trees to pick some and see. And even though the degree of difficulty barely registered, he managed to get his jersey sleeve hanked on a branch. Just at that moment a voice roared out above us, possibly from somewhere amongst the clouds. We froze. So did Bob, froze solid.

Away at the top of the Peth, where concrete steps led down into Bridgend Park, he could see the Fat Cop who kicked Ali Boompa's backside. Bob shouted a warning down to us, and without a moment's pause or thought for him marooned in the tree, we all legged it. Racing across the bridge, we saw the Fat Cop walking unhurriedly towards Bob who was already sobbing in an attempt at mitigation, and also in the hope that he might avoid tearing his jersey or being on the end of a right lifter up the backside from the officer approaching.

Screeching to a near-halt, we executed a handbrake hairpin turn down to Mayfield, a riverside lane leading round to Bullet Loan, Drying House Lane, the end of Inch Road and sanctuary, somewhere we could all claim to have been, all day, and could agree to blame it all on Bob. Bina would probably have been asleep with the paper anyway and never known I had been out. No-one was following behind us and we slowed to a relieved walk along Mayfield discussing how we could take turns to visit Bob in Borstal. Or was it Dr Barnardo's?

But when we turned into Bullet Loan, there they were. Waiting. Like Apaches on the horizon, two cops and the limp outline of Bob. He had confessed. Under interrogation, he had cracked and given the Fat Cop our names. That was it then. No option but surrender and hope that we would all be sharing a cell at the same Borstal.

'Name!' The black flip-top notebook had come out of the breast pocket and the pencil was licked and poised. I thought of pretending to be deaf and dumb, or even Peeny MacLeod, but before I opened my mouth, I saw the Fat Cop writing it down anyway.

'Address! Exact address, mind!'

So far no handcuffs had appeared and no-one had mentioned Borstal. Cobey was glaring at Bob's tear-stained face. He could have held out long enough for us to make our escape, couldn't he? Bastard. After all the names had been taken (except Bob's. Had the Fat Cop agreed to speak to the Judge?) and the note-book had its rubber band twanged around it, none of us got the usual lifter in the pants. This was clearly serious.

'Right,' said the Fat Cop, crouching down on his hunkers. Here goes. 'I should have let you eat that stuff, you stupid little buggers, and shat your pants all the way home.' And then the killer blow. 'I'll be round later to speak to your Dads.'

We trudged up Drying House Lane with Bob trailing behind. On the benches at the tennis courts, the case for the defence began. 'Right Hand up to God, Cross my Heart, and Hope to Die I never said who was with me. The Fat Cop just knew. Honest.'

'Fuck off Bob,' we all muttered. And on the way home to our certain leatherings, it began to rain and somebody said we had to go back to school soon.

At the end of one of those endless summers, I became sud-denly ill. One bright morning I woke up with a sore throat and great difficulty swallowing (which would have suited me fine if Bina had been making mince and tatties with carrots chopped in). But once I had convinced my Gran I wasn't faking (why would I? It was the school holidays), she started tickling me under the chin.

'Maybe mumps,' she said, peering at me, shaking her head as if it was my fault, 'Aye, aye, most likely mumps.' But it was only sore on one side, perhaps I just had a mump. 'Mhm, tempera-ture as well.'

By this time Cobey, Bindie, Colin and Bob had done some successful swallowing, had their breakfast and would soon be out in the street, with a whole day stretching as far as the eye could see. The August sun beat down on Inchmead Drive and maybe the tarmac would melt again.

'Back to your bed.' What? It was only my throat, I could still run and the Meadows would be crawling with Japanese snipers by now.

Much worse was to come. Much worse. Being in bed on a sunny summer morning when Cobey came to the door to see if I was coming out and hearing Bina say no was nothing compared to what she had in mind. On a saucer my Gran had mashed up butter, sugar and lemon juice, and had no intention of applying it externally. This foul paste was to be swallowed, spooned into me, whether I liked it or not. 'Now listen you to me,' demanded Bina after many attempts to push it past my pursed lips by holding my nose, 'if this is no better by dinnertime, it's the surgery for you.'

But wait, if it was sore and hard to swallow, didn't that mean that my throat wouldn't work the other way round as well, and not let me be sick if I ate that stuff?

'Do you want to see Dr Davidson?'

I swallowed the disgusting paste. Far in the distance I could hear Cobey, Bob, Bindie and Colin picking off the snipers in the lush, dense and dangerous undergrowth of the jungle.

'Say aaaah.' When Ma came home from her work at lunchtime, that was the only thing that anybody said directly to me. The rest of the discussion with Bina went on as if I wasn't there, even though it was all about my mump, or maybe my tonsils. This happened all the time in the days that followed. People I didn't know talked about me as though I was a boy in a story, not actually there, lying in bed listening to them discuss 'Him'. When I went to see Dr Davidson ('Christ, woman, he can still walk and the surgery's only round the bloody corner'), the same thing happened. Wearing a shiny metal disc on his forehead, like someone out of Dan Dare, and poking in my throat with the thin end of a long spoon, Dr Davidson didn't discuss anything with my Ma, he simply told her what was going to happen – to 'him'. And after Him had heard the word 'ambulance', he felt dizzy. Ambulance, bells ringing, swerving round corners and everything? Was Him on The Danger List? Like that boy in Morebattle with polio.

And then, through the screech of tyres and the clatter of men with stretchers, Him heard Dr Davidson clearly say the word 'hospital'. And then 'get Him in and get them taken out as soon as possible'. Definitely said that. Him was on The Danger List, no question, and he kept his eyes glued to the door of the consulting room, waiting for it to burst open and admit the men in the black uniforms with the white shoulder bags and a stretcher.

Back at 42, it was decided, while he was in the room, sitting next to those who were deciding, that Him would go to the Sick Kids in Edinburgh in the car. Edinburgh? Edinbloodyburgh! But they have hospitals in Kelso. Everyone looked round at Him and carried on where they had left off. Surely don't need to go all the way to Edinburgh, Unless, It's Really, SERIOUS. Him was put to bed early, no more butter and sugar, just the pink pills in the round red box from Dr Davidson. Dad brought the old radio up, plugged it in and set it on the bedside table so that Him could easily reach the dial. It was still light through the curtains and Him wondered if Hilversum was as far away as Edinburgh.

Looming behind high railings, like a giant version of Inch Road Infants School, the Sick Children's Hospital was not where Him wanted to be on a Saturday morning in August, but his throat was no better and still felt as though a ball of barbed wire was caught in it. At eleven o'clock in the bloody morning, this woman made Him take off all of his clothes in front of her, and she just stood there and looked, and then Him was told to put on a pair of pyjamas that were too small. Ma and Dad waited somewhere in a corridor while Him was put in a bed in a room the size of a hayshed but a lot less friendly. Everything squeaked, the floors, the beds, the doors, and when Ma and Dad finally came into the ward, they whispered all the time, seemed a bit scared of the nurses, particularly a fat one in a dark blue uniform. And then they went away, squeaking down the ward to the squeaky double doors. Went away and left me. Said something about see you on Monday night. But this was Saturday morning. I heard Ma blow her nose in the corridor, and then they were gone. Gone.

But before Him could get out of the bed to go after them, get back home right away, they all started to arrive. More doctors than Him had ever seen, even more than in St Swithin's Hospital in the Doctor films, came and stood around the bed, cutting off any escape route. And while the fat nurse in the dark blue uniform stared at me (and I stared back), they did it again: talked about me as if I was in another room. And what seemed like a very short time after they trooped off down the squeaky ward, two nurses and a man with a trolley came up to my bed.

Instead of telling me that it was all a mistake really, one of the nurses said that my operation would be happening soon, that I would have an injection that wouldn't hurt much, and that – they were going tosticktheneedleinmybum. They called it bottom. Which was worse. Just as she finished saying all this, the nurse grabbed my head and crushed it into her bosom while the other one yanked down my pyjama trousers. Something hard stuck into my eye, a fob-watch or a badge, and I forgot to yell when the needle was shoved into my bottom.

Much later, when my eyelids unglued themselves, nothing was familiar, not my body, the ceiling, the smell, the sounds or most of all my head. And my throat was on fire. For a long time no-one talked to me, and I had the overwhelming sense that I wasn't really there, that if I got up and walked down the squeaky ward, no-one would see me. And when I caught the bus to Kelso in my pyjamas, I wouldn't have to pay because I was invisible. That sense of absence seemed to last a long time, the hours passing into evening and perhaps beyond. And when a nurse came over to my bed, she told me that it was suppertime. Would I like something to eat? I was famished, Bina would have been proud of me, but when they propped me up on the pillows and slid a tray on to the table, all I saw was some vile beetroot slices, lettuce, tomato and a pile of crisps around the edges. When I said that I couldn't eat the crisps and didn't like the rest, the nurse became immediately irritated and whipped the plate away, leaving me only a glass of milk.

I grew to hate the hospital. It was much worse than the worst days of school and the strict regime, the immobility and the constant shaming business of being made to undress in front of other people made me count the minutes until my release.

'Well,' said the fat nurse in the navy blue uniform, 'that's you then young man! You can go home today.' What? How? How could I get home? Kelso was nearly fifty miles away and I had no money for the bus. More terrifying, I had no idea where I was, where the Sick Kids Hospital was in Edinburgh. The windows were too high to see out of and when I was allowed to go for a pee in a toilet like a normal person, there was nothing to be seen but rows of grey houses in an anonymous street. So when the time came for them to take me to the front door in my pyjamas (my Ma had taken my clothes back to Kelso) I'd have to remember that they weren't mine and promise to send them back in the post, in a parcel, when I finally got home. But where was the SMT bus station? Did Edinburgh have one with an office where you could ask about buses to Kelso, and where they'd believe you if you explained that you had no money but promised to pay it all back, so much a week from your pocket money? My Ma didn't have the phone and didn't know anybody who had. Did telegrams cost a lot? If it started to rain, my slippers would soon get really wet.

'Don't worry,' said my Ma when they came for me at last, 'you haven't missed any schooldays.'

In the autumn, before the clock-change cut short the long evenings, we tried to lengthen the school holidays by lying about homework and flying out of the kitchen door the minute after tea was cleared, before too many questions hovered. At least Cobey and the others did. I never seemed to have any homework. I wouldn't have done it anyway.

The lampposts in Inchmead Drive had been converted to electricity and whoever switched them on must have been living in Lapland because they were always lit well before gloaming began to fill in the shadows. The one at the top of our street, in the bit where cars could turn around without having to go up on the pavement, nevertheless acted as a focus for us to flit around, even on fine evenings. We scuffed at the kerbside, leaning against the lamppost, hands in pockets, not saying much, Cobey trying out a Mick McManus headlock on a complaining Colin, Bindie with his fist at his mouth doing a whispering Kent Walton commentary. It seemed that television and films were beginning to supply us with a new (and precise) lexicon of adjectives.

'Chasey!' It was only a matter of time before somebody said it. 'Let's play chasey.' Gloaming was the best time, the half-dark of shape shifting when no-one could be quite sure of what they might have seen out of the corner of an eye. A bit like a loose combination of hide-and-seek and tig, chasey had no fixed rules and all it really involved was one group of whooping little boys waiting for an agreed interval and then chasing another, silent, shushing group until they could find and overpower them. Inchmead Drive (except for the gardens), the Poorhouse, the horsefield, the big laundry on Inch Road and the vastness of the rugby ground compassed our hunting grounds for chasey.

The grandstand was especially grand. Built entirely out of wood, with beams inside it broad enough to lie flat and invisible on, it held endless, adrenalin possibilities. Best was to climb high enough in the infrastructure to be out of sight from the ground and well over the heads of the pursuing group when they inevitably came clattering in, looking, exasperated, suddenly whispering when a pigeon blattered into the air. Once Bob Thompson leaned over a beam and gobbed perfectly on Cobey's head and I covered Bindie McCombie with a blizzard of sand.

If girls were out after tea and they gathered beside us under the yellow glow of the lamppost, then we played Truth, Dare, Double Dare, Promise or Repeat because it was embarrassing. A series of challenges, the game always developed into gender warfare. If a boy said a sentence or a word, the girl opposite had to repeat it exactly, no matter how dirty it was. Suzie Smith had to say 'I've got big tits' when she didn't have any, and I was double-dared (maybe it was triple because it was so bad) to take out my willie and show it to Violet Taylor. Nobody else saw it, just Violet, and while it is true to say that she was interested (otherwise why did she double-dare me?), she wasn't very impressed and would never have dreamed of touching it.

Bob Thomson reckoned that women had milk in their busts. 'Don't be daft.' There followed a long, contemplative silence as we walked down Edenside Road to the first day at the Abbey School. 'What's it for?' On this particular point Bob was uncertain but absolutely sure that brassières were worn to stop it pouring down their fronts. For days afterwards I stared at women's busts looking for signs of dampness, but never saw a thing.

The Abbey School presented more mysteries. The handicrafts class got Mrs Blacklie and she was keener on singing than raffia mats.

'Step we gaily on we go! Heel for heel and toe for toe! Arm in arm and row on row! All for Mairi's wedding!'

Because I refused to sing these and other baffling songs, Mr Bonsor was sent for.

'But I can't sing.'

'That's no excuse. Everyone can sing.'

He made me stand up in front of the whole class and sing something which began, 'Boney was a warrior. Way, Ay, Aa.' Boney? Was it a dog? And when I hissed at Terror Scott to fuck off for sniggering in the front row, that was the end of the recital for Mr Bonsor and Mrs Blacklie. Far worse than being dragged into the Headmaster's study for a dose of the tawse, I was given a letter for my Ma and Dad.

At 42 nobody spoke to me after Ma had opened it. My parents went off down to the bottom of the garden while Bina and I just looked at each other. 'You're really going to get it in a minute,' said Barbara with undisguised anticipation. But when they came back in nothing happened. No row, no leathering, just Ma with a real granite face and Dad sitting in the living room, making a lot of noise with pages of the *Scotsman*. This was psychological warfare, much worse than a leathering. I had no idea what was simmering under the surface, only that it wasn't good. And just before bed, 'Now listen you to me,' said Ma, 'Speak to no-one at school tomorrow. Put on clean shorts and a shirt. And bloody well behave yourself.'

At 3 p.m. we were to see Mr Scrimgeour in his study. Apparently there were Special Schools really bad kids were sent away to, like being in the army, except in prison as well, but no rifles. And it was much worse than Borstal or Dr Barnardo's. Perhaps Mr Scrimgeour could make you go there for telling Terror Scott to fuck off. Maybe that was enough. Sign a chit and that was it. Lying in my bed going over the range of bad things I knew about (what else could there be?) it occurred to me that if I held my breath long enough under the covers, I could die. Commit suicide. And that would spite them all, Mrs Blacklie and Mr bloody Bonsor and Miss MacRae. Mr Smeaton could do a cheap little headstone for a neighbour and there wouldn't be much carving to do since I hadn't lived all that long. And I'd leave a note to get him to put 'He died just because he couldn't sing'. That would show them.

Outside Mr Scrimgeour's office my Ma spat on her hankie to rub some of the grime off my wobbly cheeks, fussed with my hair and told me to breathe through my nose so as not to look so gormless. I had recently begun to eat everything Bina set in front of me and put on a series of growing spurts which made me much taller than most of my classmates. In between stretching up, I became very roly-poly with bloodhound cheeks and a sticking-out stomach. Which is how I looked in the class photo for that year. I doubt if gormless quite covered it. Ma was wearing a rain-coat and the same granite expression from the night before.

I remember no details from the interview with Mr Scrimgeour, except that it was about Him again. While I sat on a chair by the wall remembering to breathe through my nose, Ma was on the other side of his desk. She seemed to do most of the talking and he said hardly anything at all. If he had mentioned Special Schools or Borstal or prison, that would have registered, but the Headmaster just seemed to nod for much of the time as Ma spoke quietly to him. At the end of the interview they both stood up and shook hands in the doorway. And when we left the office I managed to stand on Mr Scrimgeour's toes.

It was as though Ma had waved a magic wand. Instead of being sent away or leathered or having to promise never to swear in Mrs Blacklie's class ever again, I was to go into the A class. The A class. After the holidays, I was to start in Miss Turnbull's class with all the nice children. And if I gave her any cheek, or refused to sing, or do any damned thing I was told to do, then I was for the high jump. No question. And when Ma said things like that, she got awful quiet, and I listened very carefully indeed.

Years later I asked her what she had said to Mr Scrimgeour. 'Oh nothing much. I just told him that your sisters did well at the school, that your Dad and I weren't stupid and that you just couldn't be. It was all in there and it was the school's job to get it out.'

What she really did was to show that she believed me, not them, believed in me, not in their judgement. I was too young to do more than intuit what my Ma had done, but I knew it was different, completely unexpected. And on that day, in the Headmaster's study, she changed my life in the clearest demonstration of steadfast love that any child could hope for. My Ma fought for me and we both won.

It had legs that screwed in the bottom and optional doors to keep out the dust, and at 7/6d a week the rent was not cheap, but the mahogany finish looked posh. The first night we had the telly is a pungent memory. Aerials were being attached to almost every chimney on our council estate as rental agreements and better technology quickly created a mass audience.

'The next Tonight will be tomorrow night. Goodnight,' said Cliff Michelmore. What? Mouth open, I was baffled, awed and avid for more. Derek Hart, Fyfe Robertson (was it an ulcer?), Geoffrey Johnson-Smith, Alan Whicker, Polly Elwes and a calypso from Cy Grant. At 42 no-one spoke when the credits rolled. I expected the optional doors to close and Auld Jean to appear from the kitchen with a tray of tubs and choc ices. Even Bina watched it for a bit before going back to looking out of the living room window.

Then there was more. Jaunty music, and Phil Silvers as Sergeant Bilko. Bilko, Elwes, Michelmore? Even the names were exotic. And what was a motorpool? Who cares? And then a huge sigh, a big close-up of a sad man announcing 'It's HHHHHancock's Half Hour.' *Panorama* with Richard Dimbleby, one hand in his jacket pocket. And then, and then, my sisters and I hiding behind the sofa, barely able to watch, *Quatermass and the Pit*. It felt like the wide world had arrived on one single evening, brought to us in a big box in the back of one of Bob Swan's vans. As everyone fiddled with the vertical hold and turned up the contrast, Inchmead Drive was deserted. *Boots and Saddles* was nothing compared to *Tonight* with Cliff Michelmore. And who was it who kept phoning him while he was on the telly? Was his tea ready?

A while after we found the BBC on the dial, my Dad came across The Other Side by accident, while he was fiddling about trying to improve reception. Tyne-Tees Television from Newcastle was the nearest ITV station to Kelso and the Tweed Valley, but sometimes it seemed very distant. From the Pontop Pike transmitter, we could also get BBC North East. The nightly regional news programme, *Look North*, turned out to be 'Look South' for us and although it once mentioned the new bus station in Berwick-Upon-Tweed, it made us feel as if we lived in a blank part of the map, an empty quarter, an in-between place where nothing much ever happened, certainly nothing important enough to be on the telly. ITV was just as remote and its only real connection with Kelso took place when Tyne Tees TV was switched off and people went down the street to get some items of shopping, what Bina called 'the messages'. 'Murraymints! Murraymints! The Too-Good-To-Hurry-Mints' were available at Baikie's sweetie shop and at Massey the Chemist you could buy tubes of 'PepsoDENT, PepsoDENT. You'll wonder where the yellow went when you brush your teeth with PepsoDENT!' Marjie liked the adverts better than the programmes on ITV.

Suddenly Bina started to give me money. Not to keep or spend on myself but for going down the street for the messages after school if anything was needed or had run out in one of the daily vans. My Ma couldn't do it, especially if what was short was something needed for my Dad's tea, because she was at her work. In the Fifties and early Sixties, before telephones came into the lives of ordinary people, your time at work was not to be interupted by items of personal business, it belonged to whoever was paying. Once there, you were virtually incommunicado, on another planet, somebody else's planet. The only time a family member or a neighbour went to see anybody while they were at their work was when someone had died. Like the time Ella McIlroy's husband Tam fell down dead in the SMT bus station. Otherwise, from 8 a.m. until 5 p.m. you were at your work and therefore beyond ordinary contact. And Barbara couldn't go for the messages any more because she always had swotty, speccy homework to do so that she could keep on beating speccy Roy McConachie and come first in the class, again. And Bina's corns were so bad that she needed both hands to walk.

So I was reluctantly given a torn-off corner of the *Scotsman* with a spidery list of messages and a wee bit more than the exact money. The Store always had everything Bina had scribbled down and I never went to the posh grocers' shops in Kelso Square, the places where the toffs parked their bronchitic Land Rovers. You could tell a toff a mile away. Even in the summer they wore wellies and thought it was OK to go into the town for the messages wearing them, even into shops to buy whatever toffs ate for their tea. And they walked differently from us, slow, relaxed, straight-backed, like they owned the place. Which they did. But most of all you could tell a toff a mile away because you could hear them before you saw them. The noise they made was unavoidable. Some of them talked so loud that everyone around them was reduced to whispering and getting out of the road fast. Toffs just didn't care if other people knew what their messages were, the concept of a black affront never squeezed in between the braying, and when one toff met another one in Kelso Square, they talked as though they were standing three fields away from each other. And their clothes made Ethel and Doddie look like millionaires: elbows out their jumpers, corduroy trousers without the corduroy and bunnets bought in another age.

Toffs never went into the Store, perhaps they weren't allowed, perhaps it was the one place they didn't own. By the time I had wandered down to Roxburgh Street, Bina's list had crumpled around the half crown she had put into the pocket of my shorts 'so I know it went in and there's no holes'. And when I reached the broad brown counter where the scales and the cheesecutter sat, I just took it out and handed it all over to the man with the white apron tied up under his armpits.

'Now then,' he spread the torn bit of the *Scotsman* flat on the counter, 'that's sugar is it? Or suet maybe?'

I shook my head. What's suet?

'Well, what's for your tea?'

Dunno. Don't care. The man leaned over the counter down to my eyeline. 'Don't know much, do you?'

No, not bloody much. Bugger off buggerlugs. Fat jobbie yourself.

He started to cut, pour and count out the other things on

Bina's indecipherable list, taking an empty, flat white packet from under the counter and setting it open on the balance. Against a round brass weight on the other plate, he carefully poured white powdery stuff into the packet until it slowly eased down to become level. Then he looked at me for a moment, whipped it off and in a blur of deftness folded the top and stuck it down with sellotape. Currants were weighed out with a scoop. Sweaty yellow cheese was magically sliced with a wire and folded in crackling tissue and a small tin of Royal baking powder plonked down next to the packets. 'Must be sugar. She's doing fruit scones.'

The man in the apron handed over a penny and slid me a small cardboard box with the messages inside and a slip for the Divi Book tucked into the top of a packet. I'd refused to take a shopping bag like a jessie. Bina knew the price of everyday items precisely and her calculation had allowed me a penny for a sweetie to be sucked up the road home. Mrs Baikie didn't seem to mind extended browsing as long as you didn't breathe on the trays of delights. A Highland Toffee with a picture of a hairy cow on the wrapper was good and it could be made to last all the way back to 42, but once it was in your gob, it stuck there, and it was too small and hard to break into two bits so that you could save one for after. Halfpenny chews the colour of the Roxy's decor just fizzed into nothing before you had turned the corner into Union Street. Licorice laces lasted though and could be quickly bitten off and pocketed if Cobey or Bindie happened into view.

At about the same time as I was trusted with money and the messages my Ma began to fill up all the corners in my life. One evening she took me down the street to the Carnegie Library to see Mr Bird. Peering over the lending counter through National Health tortoiseshell specs, the old librarian looked at me like a kindly owl, cocking his head to one side.

'What about a Richmal Crompton?' he asked.

Who? I looked at Ma. It might have been a cricket bat or a make of bicycle for all I knew. Instead it was a Just William story about his weedy little gang called the Outlaws, a girl named Violet Elizabeth Bott and someone known as Hubert Lane. Even though the worst they ever did was stick out their tongues at each other, they reckoned themselves to be really bad. I kept expecting them to meet the Famous Five and Julian to give them a jolly good talking to. Or hoping for Ernie Woodhead, 'Fuck off William Arsehole.'

Truth is that I didn't much care, having lost my urge to join the English Middle Classes for tea, somewhere in Kent, near a cricket ground. But I did start reading, two or three books a week, and particularly Scottish history, and true stories about some really hard people who actually lived some time in the past, some of them near Inchmead Drive.

I mostly read in bed and Dad rigged up a small lamp that clipped on to the headboard of my bed. It lit my imagination. In the pool of secret light, I found myself transported. Through the pages of many books I discovered worlds to visit, people to walk beside, dangers to face, dreams to inhabit and revelations to wonder at. Most of all books taught me that I was not unique, alone, or stupid. And that even when life at 42 Inchmead Drive seemed everyday grey, sparkle could be found between their covers.

When Sputniks began to orbit the Earth, reality merged with metaphor and it became clear that there really were other worlds to visit. Russian cosmonauts and American astronauts would soon visit Venus and see if Dan Dare was right about the Treens, the green people, the Venutians who lived like plants amongst the planets. And when John Glenn followed Yuri Gagarin into space and we could all understand what was going on, because Houston was telling us, in space-English, what we were looking at on the telly, it became clear that I had been right all along about the Reverend Falloon of Trinity North Church. He was the strangest man I ever saw. Not scary like Zeke Lillie, or threatening like Dr Davidson, just very strange. When the whole school went to a service at Trinity North, I couldn't take my eyes off him. Small, with a large bald head, specs and an unchanging expression on his face, somewhere between pain and effort, he moved very slowly and carefully, as if walking was something he had only just learned to do, something to be considered fully before each step was taken.

Like all ministers, he cast his eyes downwards as he moved towards the pulpit stair in his long black dress, and so deliberate was each step that it looked as though he had forgotten how he did the last one. But his walk and appearance were nothing compared to his voice. When he began to speak, it was never clear where the sound was coming from at first. The Reverend Falloon gave no indication it was him doing it, he didn't move anything, not his lips, his head or his arms. And the tone was always the same – flat, nasal, like something recorded, like a button had been pressed somewhere and the words came out, perhaps from behind the organ, or up out of the metal grills lining the aisles.

Until Houston talked to John Glenn, all of this strangeness remained just that, strange. But during a long school service when all of the good boys and girls read bits out of the Bible or sang in Mr bloody Bonsor's nancy choir, I worked it out. On the other six days a week when he wasn't doing anything, the Reverend Falloon went secretly to Texas, to Mission Control, to talk to the astronauts. It was definitely his voice on the telly, and if he ever had anything to do during the week (like a school service) then his specially trained double stood in and they played a recording of his voice announcing the hymns and doing the blessing part at the end. Because the reason that the Reverend Falloon was in Houston talking to spacemen in the first place was that he had been up there himself. He had come here from another planet. He knew what the astronauts would find in Outer Space, because he was an Alien from Outer Space. It was blindingly obvious, clues were everywhere. First of all ministers were always talking about Up There, some of them as if they had visited a few times and had a look round. And how could a minister from Kelso possibly go to Houston, Texas every week *unless* he had some incredibly important things to tell them. And even more obvious, he actually looked like an Alien. Most weeks in the *Eagle* Dan Dare and Digby had trouble with the Enemy of Mankind, the Evil Mekon, and even though he was green, like the Treens, he did look very, very like the minister of Trinity North Church. Mission Control obviously believed that the American astronauts would encounter the Mekon sooner or later, and who better to train them than a close, but much nicer, relative – the Falloon. The fact that he had no first name proved it.

Miss Turnbull had a first name. No other teacher I had come across had one, but she did. Definitely. And that meant she had a Ma and a Dad, and possibly brothers and sisters. One of the girls knew what it was because her Dad had used it, because, well, he knew her. And the reason he knew her, and this was the hardest bit to imagine, was because – he went to school with her. School. Miss Turnbull had once been young. In fact she had not only been young, she might even have gone to school in the very same old classroom we sat in. Wee Elma Turnbull.

She also had something else no other teacher had. Miss Turnbull laughed. Not a smile with a little sniggery sort of snort on the end of it, but the real thing, a big, head back, flat out laugh. And sometimes she said well done to you even though you weren't a pet or one of the cheesy pigtails in the front row. It took me a few weeks to get used to the idea that I liked Miss Turnbull, that she would help me instead of giving me rows, that she actually wanted me, me in particular, to do well, that she was on my side.

Between the three of them, Cliff Michelmore, Mr Bird and Miss Turnbull found a way to persuade me to stop refusing, and start accepting all that was being offered. In 1961, orchestrated by my Ma, education began. And at the same time something else equally revolutionary began to stir.

In Primary 7A, the girls didn't smell of pee, like Violet Taylor, and they were a lot smarter. Every time Miss Turnbull asked a question a forest of girls' hands went shooting up. Some of them even bounced up and down on their chairs, snapping their fingers, excitedly imploring, 'Please Miss. Please Miss.' Watching was a herd of clueless, bovine boys (except for James Clow) and when Miss Turnbull specifically directed a question to our side of the classroom, it could take·a while.

Girls also seemed to understand something boys didn't. In contrast to our slack-jawed amazement at almost everything, what girls understood was simple and crucial. They knew what would happen next. In fact some of the really clever ones knew what would happen several nexts ahead. To me the world was full of surprises.

Allied to all this cerebration were clothes, and especially frocks. In contrast to the grazing ruminants on the boys' side of Miss Turnbull's class, girls dressed with a growing realisation that it was important and enjoyable. Some of them liked their new frocks so much they used to brush and swish the skirts with their arms as they walked up the road home. Frocks had cardies to match, pigtails and ponytails had ribbons to match them and white ankle socks matched everything. Boys sometimes forgot to finish dressing and undone flies triggered a sniggering buzz but rarely any helpful pointing. And missed-out latches at the back meant that stripy snake-belts failed to hold up shorts, which could be revealing. One of the biggest problems with them in the summer was their colour. All of us wore long-legged light khaki shorts, like the 8th Army at El Alamein, and even if things went only slightly wrong in the boys' toilets, it was very embarrassing. Sometimes when even the smallest drop fell on the crotch area, it changed the colour from light khaki to dark and could spread alarmingly in moments, like ink on blotting paper.

Hygiene was in fact optional for boys, unless you wanted to go for a walk round the racecourse with May Johnstone. For reasons which were unclear to me at the time, and astonishing to Bina, I began to wash regularly. And wait until every last drop had dripped out and check that my flies were done up when I came back to the classroom from the boys' toilet.

'Em. Er, do you want to go, em, for, em, awalkroundthe-racecourse?' I caught up with May Johnstone on the way up home from school.

'Don't you be cheeky!'

She was (and remains) very pretty, with melting doe-eyes, long brown hair, and a bust. Doggedness worked – truth be told I followed May like a persistent bloodhound until at last she sighed and agreed to come with me for a walk round the race-course. When we reached the point furthest from the town, we came on a large patch of long grass. May knew what would happen next. Which was good, because I had only the vaguest of ideas. We lay down beside each other and once we were as comfortable as dry, hummocky ground allowed and safely out of the sight of everyone except those in passing aircraft, I held her hand. For ages. No-one spoke. Nothing else happened. My instincts were revving in neutral, certain I should do something quick, before May announced it was time to go home for tea, but I had no idea what.

'What's it for?' I asked.

'What?'

'Your brassière. What's it for?'

'Don't be dirty!'

'Does it keep it all in? No leaks?'

'My tea'll be ready.'

After more walks round the racecourse, some discussion on the acceptable way to do kissing, I finally, hesitantly, put my hand on her bust. My right hand. Expecting May to fly off in outrage or fetch me a haymaker round the ear, I was very tentative. Perhaps she hadn't noticed. But she knew what would happen next. Nothing. May lay quite still and continued to stare up at the blue sky from our patch of hay. Thereafter I clamped my hand to her young breast with a solemn passion that drew its dull flame from imitation rather than anything spontaneous. We were waiting for the world to begin.

FIVE

The Beginning of the World

'FRANCE MUST BE some place, really great.'

Bob Thompson and I were sitting under the grandstand at the Poynder Park rugby ground.

'Why? What's so great about France?' I balanced myself on a broad wooden beam while Bob scuffed his shoes in the litter-strewn dust.

'Well, they've got everything you need, haven't they?'

The stand had an unlocked door to its innards and on summer nights it supplied cover for ardent and probably illicit lovers.

'What?'

In the dust we had often found discarded little packets and once a trophy to fire a dozen puberty-stricken dreams – a pair of lacy black knickers. Knickers ripped down one side.

'French Letters of course. FLs. You know. French, like. And it's where French Kissing was first invented, isn't it?'

Bob was right. France was where they had sex sorted out. Knew what they were doing. Brigitte Bardot seemed to be about to do nothing else except, well, it. She just looked that way. Lucille Ball, on the other hand, or Victor Mature were definitely not doing anything like that, and Charlton Heston had been in at least two films where God had some lines. Or Finlay Currie did. But French films and film stars were on about something else. And French influence was everywhere when it came to, you know, it, even reaching right under the rugby club stand where we regularly came across used FLs in the dust. Bindie McCombie speared one with a sharp stick once and chased us across the pitch waving it in the air.

There was sometimes a strange smell under the stand, particularly in the cubicle at the corner where a man sold tickets on a Saturday afternoon. That was where we found the knickers. And it was clearly none other than the smell of it, a mixture of perfume and yuk.

'You definitely have to lie down to do it.' Cobey had seen photographs. 'And the man lies on top of the woman.'

'Definitely.'

A close forensic examination of the dusty floor in the ticket cubicle revealed no female body prints but we did keep an eye open for women with dark smudges on the backs of their frocks. This was important. We knew plenty of sixteen-year-old boys who had definitely done it, but no girls who had. We wanted to see what one looked like. Were they different? How different? Did they begin to walk differently after they had done it? Were they the former owners of a pair of black lacy knickers, badly ripped?

We depended entirely on observation when it came to girls. It was inconceivable that a boy and a girl could share information, could talk about doing it, what it was like, how you did it, or anything at all to do with it. Girls just couldn't. If they did, it meant that they had done it, or wanted to do it. Which was probably worse. In any case all the girls in my class were only interested in the sophisticates in the year above. In Primary 7, where there was no option, they had suffered enough of our lugubrious, bovine fumblings, but now the long grass around the summer racecourse grew undisturbed.

More worryingly, some of the girls in our class were not girls. On the first day of term two women turned up, from St Boswells. Sheelagh Drummond and Sandra Black were allegedly the same age as myself and the other dishevelled herbivores, but they appeared at Kelso High School as though they were time travellers from another galaxy. Both had hairdos, busts and wore stockings instead of ankle socks. Throughout the eternities of double-period maths or science I stared at Sheelagh and Sandra, watching their every movement, how they smoothed their pleated skirts under their behinds before they sat down and pulled down the hem after they had. How they daintily replaced each pencil or pen in their paisley pattern pencil-case and zipped it up every time. How they stretched out their fingers to check their fingernails. How they carried their schoolbags that weren't schoolbags in front instead of looping their arms through knapsack-style. I failed O-grade maths twice and never got the hang of science.

I used to wash my hair after rugby and that was usually it for the week. Same with the other ruminants. As for haircuts, Jinx Thomson the Barber just did the one style. No point in asking, once you were in the chair staring in slack-jawed depression at the item in mirror with the nylon sheet wrapped around, that was it. Short back and sides. Without any preliminaries Jinx got going with his hand clippers that tore out as much hair as they cut and after five minutes you looked like a new recruit to *The Army Game*.

'Anything on it?'

A splurge of white Brycreem or Silvikrin was squirted out of a large dispenser and plastered on before Jinx combed the greasy mess forward, decided on a parting and shed the longer stuff either side. Once out on the street my head always felt very cold, even in summer.

Sheelagh Drummond and Sandra Black on the other hand had proper, well-thought-out hairdos: backcombed, even washed every other day, bits curled down like female sideboards, fringes that never moved in the wind. The result of time spent in front of the mirror – every morning. These were women and as such almost totally unattainable. The only thing I could think of that might elevate me above the herd was shaving. Because that's what second-year boys and real men did. And so, completely unnecessarily for a fair-headed sort, I started shaving, scarting my Dad's Gillette safety razor across my downy chin and cutting a straight line under my wispy sideboards. At least I didn't have any spots to decapitate. Even so, the effects of needless shaving were painful and invisible but they made me feel better.

What made me feel worse was the undoubted fact that in addition to their hairdos, Sheelagh and Sandra were both clever, owning a withering, quickfire wit. After months of attrition and shaving, I finally managed to persuade Sandra Black to catch the bus from St Boswells to provincial Kelso to come to the church youth club dance with me. In the same hall where years before Mrs Boles had unpacked the nuances of catholic dogma I did the twist with Sandra Black, glaring at any other member of the herd who shuffled close to her, threatening to ask her to dance.

Blowing out my cheeks and repeatedly drawing the back of my hand across my forehead, I suggested to Sandra that it was very warm indeed in this badly ventilated hall. Phew. Stifling. Andwouldyouliketogooutsideforawhile? Possibly. She smiled at me and twisted a bit more of the night away with Chubby Checker, or Chris Montez, or whoever the bloody hell it was. Even when the slow numbers came up all the lights stayed on, and all I could think of was the Famous Five. And, well, it was getting really, really warm. Phew. Finally Sandra took my hand and led me out of the hall like it was her idea. Fine. OK.

Outside it was mobbed, couples leaning against every perpendicular surface, definitely no lying down going on. After a feverish stroll across the grass, not easy for wee Sandra in her high heels, we found a space with a view across the river. With my arm around her shoulder we stared into the middle distance for a while. Neither of us spoke. I adjusted my arm. Sandra was petite, even in her tottering heels. Then I coughed a couple of times, swung round and downwards and kissed her on the forehead.

'Missed,' she said.

'Sorry, sorry, sorry about that.'

'Did you think I was taller?'

Hairdos and busts were explicable. You sort of knew why they looked good, but stockings remined a mystery. They looked good too, but why? When one of the girls in Class 1A inadvertently revealed a stocking top during a lesson the news electrified the normally somnolent herbivores. Boys pointed, nudged other boys, widened their eyes and nodded their heads towards the revelation. Why? Thighs weren't everything. In fact girls' thighs were nothing special at all, in view regularly on the hockey pitch, PT periods, below swimsuits. What was it about the sight of a few inches of thigh above a stocking top that seemed shocking? And which still seems to stir a bovine grunt from gentlemen of a certain age. Who knows? But like the rest of the boys in 1A, I was stirred.

After I missed and kissed her forehead Sandra Black chucked me. Probably for incompetence. And Sheelagh Drummond was going out with Kenny Lowson who was two years older than me, cheerful, good-looking, a heavy shaver and from St Boswells. Even though I went to the St Boswells youth club dance I couldn't get near Sheelagh. Brian bloody Wilson danced with her for the whole evening (where was Kenny Lowson? was he ill? was it over between them? had he severed an artery while shaving?) with both of them holding a big red balloon between them and laughing a great deal. I was baffled. Sex was no laughing matter and everyone knew that women only went for serious guys with firm, clenched jawlines who were really hard and didn't say much. But these two were dancing around, up on the stage, with this big bloody balloon, laughing, tickling each other and having what looked a lot like fun.

'Hello.' Beep, beep, beep, beep, clunk. 'Hello. Hello. Emmm, Mrs Drummond? Hello. Is Sheelagh there please?'

The phone box in Inch Road was like a greenhouse, it smelt of disinfectant, and the sweat poured down my brow as I checked my hair in the little mirror next to the 999 instructions. 'Hello.

Sheelagh? ... Who? ... No, it's not. It's me. Alistair Moffat ...
No? ... Oh, OK then ... Right you are then ... Sorry to bother
you. Bye.'

After half a dozen breathless sweaty appeals to a number in St
Boswells, Sheelagh relented and invited me to her birthday party.
I arrived two hours early. Having spotted me loitering in the
street, her Dad got me to help with the chairs and taking up the
carpet in the sitting room. We discussed what to do if the record
player got knocked or the needle jumped out of the grooves
during the twist. When the hall table needed shifting I could
hear Sheelagh whispering to her mother at the top of the stairs.
She didn't seem in a birthday mood. And then Kenny Lowson
arrived to give her Dad a hand. Perhaps they compared notes on
different sorts of razors while I helped her Mum in the back
kitchen. After the party started I went to sit on the garden wall
for a while.

Love just wasn't working out. And sex seemed even more
remote. All of these women-girls were worlds away from the
glamour of Brigitte Bardot and it, and even further distant from
the dusty seediness of FLs under the rugby club stand. On the
garden wall I came to a resolution. I resolved to be cautious and
to serve a proper apprenticeship. If Sandra Black thought I was
feckless and Sheelagh Drummond wouldn't go out with me,
then who would?

Back in the party the record player was only playing slow
numbers. As Sheelagh's Dad had predicted, anything more vig-
orous had made the needle jump and scratch the discs. But none
of the shuffling couples were complaining. 'Venus in blue jeans,
Mona Lisa with a pony tay, ay ayl' ... Bobby Vee sounded good
and Janet Armstrong wasn't dancing. Would she? She would. She
did. And in an unprecedented surge of courage I kissed her, for
at least a minute. Eyes tight shut, lips pursed tighter. In 1962
duration was everything, and tongues were for talking. But it was
great. Janet even smiled at me, seemed keen, wasn't on the
phone, but would definitely come with me to the first year hop

But because these were the first pieces of music I was encouraged to listen to, was told were for me, this medley of hardy standbys for Uncle Mac's Family Favourites is still playing in a secret part of my memory, planted there despite the fact that I could easily picture the Famous Five sitting by the fire, passing around a box of chocs, with stupid smirking smiles on their stupid faces. Listening to Nellie the Elephant packing her trunk (very funny) to say goodbye to the circus. Or with a waddle and a quack, the stupid Ugly Duckling leaving town (they didn't live in bloody towns) all furry and brown. Or something. Most of the Families that Uncle Mac played Favourites for seemed to be with the British Army on the Rhine (was Hitler's wee brother still holding out?) and certainly not living at 42 Inchmead Drive.

But Adam Faith, Billy Fury and Susan Maugham were playing at the first year dance, not appearing, just playing on the p.a. system. Perhaps because I intuited that these and many others were largely British versions of something essentially American, and because I knew that Frank Hawker and his black leather gang played 'What do ya wan if ya don't wan money? What do ya wan if ya doan wan dough? Tell me what it is an I'll give it to ya, honey' all the time on the juke box in the Spin-a-Disc café, it never felt like my music either, always somebody else's. Adam Faith and Billy Fury looked hard, had firm jawlines, and probably didn't say much, like real men. Older girls quite fancied Billy (I never came across anybody who was keen on Adam Faith) and Janet Armstrong thought Cliff Richard was cute. But when he went off on a Summer Holiday, no more worries for a week or two, with the Shadows and Una Stubbs, it was more like the Famous Five when bad things almost happened but didn't in the end, and not at all like *The Dangerous Years* when somebody who looked a bit like Victor Mature got himself and his girlfriend in a lot of trouble with the cops in somewhere that might have been Blackpool. Tame, seemingly under adult control, stuck in Tin Pan Alley (where?), popular music of the very early 1960s did not belong to or grow out of the excitements of real young people. People not like Una Stubbs. It came from somewhere else.

Dancing remained an unresolved issue. Slow numbers were fine. They involved pressing up against a girl as hard as possible, and then swaying a bit and shuffling. But anything more animated could quickly descend into hilarity, for no obvious reason, and not only despatch a partner back to the rows of chairs along the walls but also permanently discourage all of her pals who were sniggering at the epileptic gyrations performed to a rhythm playing in only your head. When Chubby Checker pioneered the twist, he solved some of my particular problems. Even though he was a bit before my time at the first year hop, I was able to adapt the basic grinding-out-a-cigarette-on-the-sidewalk step with enough side-to-side movement to avoid solecism, or at least give me the benefit of the doubt. It helped if I hunched up my shoulders like Billy Fury and moved my hands in time to the music in a variety of pointing gestures. It must have worked because instead of bursting out laughing Janet Armstrong agreed to come outside immediately I shouted (at the precise moment a record ended and a dead silence began) the invitation.

'Christ almighty, will you look at the state of that!' my Dad was excited. 'What are they like? Bloody disgrace. Short back and sides would sort out that lot. Bring back National bloody Service.'

Sunday Night at the London Palladium didn't usually get him so worked up, but in early 1963 it was an exciting show. The only person in the living room who wasn't excited was Bina. She was amazed, not watching the telly but staring at us all in amazement while we stared at John, Paul, Ringo and George playing their way through 'Please Please Me', 'Whoa yeh, like I please you'. Shaking his head, blowing out his cheeks, my Dad heckled the Beatles throughout their performance, and even at the bit at the end of the show when they reappeared with all the other artists on the bill, standing on a slow revolve waving to the audience, the wings and the back wall of the stage.

I was embarked on forming a deep and uncomplicated relationship with John Lennon. I wanted to be him. Each night in front of the bathroom mirror I tilted my head back to check on hair growth and sucked in my cheeks to create a pair of Lennon-like dimples. Days after it was released I had run down the street to Bob Swan's to buy 'Please Please Me' for 6/8d on the Parlophone label, please. We didn't have a record player, but that detail was less important than owning an actual Beatles record, being part of whatever it was that was happening.

As more and more music from the Searchers, the Rolling Stones, the Fourmost, the Swinging Blue Jeans, Billy J. Kramer washed over us, it was clear that the world was no longer moving in a sedate and dignified direction set by Richard Dimbleby or even Cliff Michelmore (God knows what Fyfe Roberston made of it all). Tens of thousands of young people screamed, rushed, crushed against barriers wherever the Beatles went as they led us out of post-war Britain and on to somewhere else that looked like a lot more fun.

And real people began to appear on television. Not only were the members of the groups themselves largely unacquainted with the Famous Five (except maybe the Dave Clark Five) or with What Katy Did Next, those who were buying and listening to their records turned out to be like us, even if we didn't understand them when they talked. Janice on *Thank Your Lucky Stars* spoke with such an impenetrable Birmingham accent ('Oi loik the backingggg. Oil geeve eet foive') that Brian Matthew had to interpret for the nation. But there she was, one of us, on the telly, in a short skirt, every week, deciding what was good and what was not. And Janice knew her stuff, despite the fact that her alphabet contained fifty more vowels than ours.

Suddenly it seemed that young people were no longer younger old people wearing suits, sports jackets, stringy ties and drip-dry Bri-nylon shirts. As a million bathroom mirrors confirmed, hair was growing longer by the week, sales of Brylcreem and Silvikrin were plummeting and Jinx Thomson's clientele shrinking, slinking off round to Bridge Street where Len Henry had daringly employed a young lady to cut gents' hair, and, and, she had been a finalist in the Miss Kelso beauty competition. Young people began to ignore disapproval and look very different. Jeans, clean jeans mind you, were accepted as going-out wear and rapidly rising hemlines began to usher in a wonderful but sadly short period before tights became widely available. With the Beatles everything changed, and as baby boomers raised in the late Forties and Fifties earned wages and salaries a ready market met and encouraged the explosion of music, clothes, entertainment and hair. Even *Sunday Night at the London Palladium* changed. Norman Vaughan replaced Bruce Forsyth and when all was well with the show (which was all the time) he cocked his thumb and pronounced whatever it was as 'swinging', and very occasionally worried about giving the thumbs down to anything 'dodgy'.

Ian McKirdy had a record player (it was really a radiogram and about the size of a sideboard) and we sat in his front room listening to records in a miasma of excitement. Imitation obsessed us and of course we formed a group, 'The Druids'. What mattered urgently was being on stage somewhere, anywhere, adopting the roles of John, Paul, George and Ringo and acquiring by simple transference the magic dust which had mysteriously sprinkled down on them. From forgotten sources we acquired three guitars, and also a large empty teabox and a snare drum borrowed from a member of the Boys' Brigade. In our haste to climb onstage and not so much be like our heroes as actually be them, we focused entirely on how we looked and refused to waste time learning how to play our instruments. Somehow when we were up there, the Druids would know what to do. Up where? In the Scout Hall of course, where a collection of parents and siblings waited expectantly.

With our guitars slung over our backs (a manoeuvre endlessly rehearsed in the mirror) we processed solemnly in and mounted the dusty wooden dais at the far end. Bindie McCombie sat behind the teabox bass drum and quickly checked that the nail hammered in to stop it shooting across the stage when he kicked it was securely in place. I carefully set my feet apart and leaned back a bit to look exactly like John Lennon, while Ian played left-handed like Paul and his brother, Ally, took up a convincing George Harrison crouch. All that was missing were cuban heels.

We had rehearsed the bit when Paul said 'Ah one, ah one two three' and apart from Ian learning all the words to 'Thank You Girl' off the record, absolutely nothing else. Unable to play a chord or a note, we twanged and strummed tunelessly through the song, reducing to rubble what had been a catchy enough number. The undoubted fact that, despite Mr Bonsor's assertions otherwise, I could not sing at all was less important than my ability to reproduce John Lennon's toothy smile, dimples and all, at various appropriate points in the performance.

At the end of what must have been a painful and baffling experience, the Druids bowed deeply, reslung their guitars behind their backs, and to a bemused silence from the audience, processed solemnly out of the hall. It was their only performance. Brian Epstein did not call. But none of that was remotely important. For three or four transcendent minutes we had been up there with them, been them, and understood.

In 1963 I counted up all my two bob bits, half crowns and ten bob notes before walking down the street to Bob Swan's to consider the purchase of a KB Dansette record player, so that I could finally play all the Beatles records I had bought. Of course I knew exactly how much it would cost, what colours it came in, the different styles of wood-effect finish and how many singles and LPs it could take in a stack. There was no consideration involved, I just didn't want to part with all that hard-saved cash without some ceremony. The silver collection I dumped on Bob Swan's counter came from my first regular job, and the KB Dansette (red, with a beech veneer finish) became the first substantial item I bought with my own money.

The money came from 7/6d a week for helping Tommy Pontin deliver the Store milk. How I got the coveted job has vanished from memory. Before I started at 6 a.m. on a January morning in 1963, I hadn't ever met Tommy, there had been no interview by anyone, no negotiation over pay and no information about terms and conditions. All I had to do was turn up, on time, at the depot in East Bowmont Street, and start doing it. That was it. At that time my Ma was working as a clerkess in the Store Ledger Department. Perhaps she heard that there was a job going and asked Tommy if I would do. Being her son was probably recommendation and guarantee enough.

Turning up on time was the most important part of it. If you didn't, or worse, didn't turn up at all, it could be disastrous; hundreds of homes would have no milk for their cornflakes or porridge or cups of tea, because without help Tommy took a lot longer to get through the round, to say nothing of apologising to everybody on the way. And so when the alarm crashed into my sleep at 5.30 a.m. every morning except Sunday, I was up immediately, without a moment's hesitant thought for the warm blankets, hopping from foot to foot on the freezing linoleum as I tugged on my socks (Bina knitted several pairs specially for the Store Milk), jeans, shirt, pullover and anorak. And then out the door with a slice of warm toast in my hand and straight down to the depot.

Even at that hour, in the icy depths of the winter, there were people about, up and doing. And when the sky was open, the sooty black of the night slowly turned to blue over the rooftops as I walked down Forestfield, Edenside Road and along past the police station. Once, at a high window in East Bowmont Street I saw a woman brushing her long hair as she looked out over the winter morning, and when she saw me walking below she smiled a wonderful smile and waved at me.

At the depot Tommy had already loaded most of the metal crates on to the float by 6 a.m. and was busy with all of the other bits and pieces he delivered on the round. With a black army beret, a khaki battledress jacket and a whistly, cheery demeanour, Tommy seemed always to be the same: bustling, brisk, keen to get on up the road. We started at Grovehill, a cul-de-sac of council houses where almost every door was a customer.

Each morning, just as Tommy slid the electric float into gear and nosed out into East Bowmont Street, Bindie McCombie came cycling out of the darkness for our daily rendezvous. His bike belonged to Jack Scott the Baker and the huge front basket was filled with floury bags of rolls and bread to be delivered to Grovehill and elsewhere. It was far too early to talk. Like me, Bindie almost always had the hood of his anorak up, and when we exchanged two pints of gold top for half a dozen rolls (well-fired), we nodded to each other like Trappist monks meeting for early prayers.

As I munched my rolls and lifted the two eight-pint carriers to do the doors on one side of the street, Tommy went for a crap. His Ma lived at the bottom of Grovehill and each morning he bounced back down the steps at the side of her house and said the same thing when I met him at the float. 'Two pounds lighter!' And it must have been true. Tommy was so quick with his deliveries that he easily caught me up despite the visit to his Ma and the quick cup of tea he had with her. What could slow down both of us badly was lazy customers. If a doorstep had no empties to replace full bottles out of the eight-pint carriers, that meant double empties the day after or triple the day after that. Chaos. It involved doubling back to pick up surplus empties (something all deliverers hate) with five or six in each hand, 'Not getting off the bit!' On cold winter mornings with rain or snow, that sort of waste of time numbed every finger, and if it happened in Grovehill, it made for early swearing.

The great advantage of starting there was something much needed (apart from relief for Tommy's bowels): the respite of a short trip in the warmth of the cab to the next part of the round half a mile away. The Store milk rounds comprehended the demographics of small towns like Kelso reasonably precisely. All of the new pre- and post-war council estates had their milk delivered by Tommy and me (and Jock Mallen and his boy) because their residents were members of the Store. And like all of the goods they bought (and the services, the Store did funerals), the milk counted towards the Divi (how you collected this after your funeral remained a mystery. Perhaps Mr Smeaton got it). Because the Kelso Co-operative and Wholesale Society was exactly that, a co-operative for its members, and since there were no large supermarkets to compete in those days, most working people joined as a matter of course. Each year the members enjoyed the Divi. In the front of the carbon-papered book used to record transactions, it was described as 'the distribution of surplus as dividend on purchases'. This was repaid to members in the form of credit and it made every sort of sense to buy basics, like milk, at the Store and get something back for doing so. In Kelso the posh houses got Purves' milk (it was thought to be creamier than the Store's) or milk from Legars Farm, but some of the teachers at the High School were members of the Store. And my Ma knew who they were.

The electric float made very little noise as it whirred slowly along the darkened streets, only a click and a buzz when Tommy accelerated or braked to stop. With only the clink of bottles and the trill of whistling, we seemed to fit into the early morning, not intrude. The sleepy town woke up as we dinked a pint of milk down on its doorstep, and when the float glided past, a patchwork of lights clicked on in kitchen windows and the day began to stir.

Tommy organised the round so that it ended near 42 Inchmead Drive and allowed me enough time to get changed, eat a second breakfast, get away along the road to school and continue wondering about girls. And particularly the girls in my class. The inexplicable things they said, looks they shot – I felt as though I understood nothing about them, nothing at all – except that I wanted to.

Janet Armstrong understood all too well, and she never

allowed me to get beyond stage 3. Stage 1 was getting off with a girl in the first place. This could either be a prearranged date or persuading her to go outside with you during a dance or a party. Stage 2 was kissing; pressure rather than lip or jaw movement and certainly not a flitter of a tongue involved. Stage 3 was being allowed to put your hand on a girl's bust through two layers of clothing, including a bra. And that was it. There were lots more stages apparently, but at the first year hop Janet sensibly stuck at 3, and to me that was fine. We were a stage 3 sort of couple. No hard feelings, and once I had sorted out who was next going to be attracted to my uncanny resemblance to John Lennon, we parted amicably.

Discussion about girls could sound like a mental arithmetic exercise.

'4.'

'Never! You never got to touch her bra. Never! She's always been a 3.'

The questions in the exercise hardly ever interrogated where you had been, what film was on at the Roxy or what you had done.

'How far did you get?' was answered with a number, often one subject to inflation. 5s just never happened and if they did it was a mistake or a broken bra fastening or she was unconscious or a girl who really did think that in a certain light I looked a bit like John Lennon's wee brother. Einstein's General Theory of Relativity was easier to comprehend than a 6, in fact there was some disagreement as to what a 6 actually was since there wasn't much to hold on to and even if you did, it must have been wrist-twistingly awkward. Beyond that lay territory only explored in France after some hours of French Kissing and the acquisition of French Letters. Brigitte Bardot was probably a 7, 8, 9, and a 10, but that wasn't much consolation to us in Class 1A. There was no mention of her or any of this in *Nos Voisins Français*, the text-book dished out by Mr Taylor who had, incidentally, spent a lot of time in France. However I found myself highly motivated to become fluent in French on the off-chance that Brigitte might come to Kelso for her holidays, or if I happened to bump into her in Hawick High Street. Before a verb was conjugated, I could count from *un* to *dix* in the first week.

All of this courting by numbers supplied teenage boys with the entirely illusory sense that they were somehow in charge, exercising quality control, setting the agenda for the genders. Although I made great efforts to persuade and push the arithmetic as far as I could, all power ultimately lay in the laps of the girls. And we knew it. Sex was what they let you do. Usually tacitly, which could lead to confusion. If things got too tactile and a hand strayed without silent permission, that could be emphatically that – all the humiliation of being chucked (denied of course but no-one ever believed it) and like snakes and ladders, sliding back down to the beginning. After a few rows for going too far and some restarts, a question occurred to me, one which I have never heard answered satisfactorily. If sex was something girls reluctantly put up with, what was the real reason they agreed to go out on dates with boys? Conversation?

These early encounters were often determinant. Many boys have grown into adulthood believing that sex was something women tolerated but did not really enjoy. There is a saying in the Borders that men get married in order to have sex regularly and that women have sex in order to get married. Many adult men have gone to their graves believing that. I won't. I was extremely lucky and will remain eternally in the debt of Isobel Elliot, Evelyn Johnstone and Rae Smith, the ringleader.

The Reverend M.A. MacLeod was a flame-haired, fire-and-brimstone Highland minister and a surprise choice by the Kirk Session to take the charge of St Machar's Church. His Old Testament looks and energetic preaching might have suited a congregation in Lewis or Inverness where they enjoy that sort of thing, but in Kelso many resented his disturbing a peaceful Sunday morning when they were minding their own business in the back pews, handing round the pandrops. But MacLeod did have one progressive idea. In the crypt of his huge kirk a youth club opened. Two evenings a week we could play our records, buy squash, lemonade and crisps, and play table tennis. And talk to girls. One winter night in 1964 the heavens moved into a unique configuration. Perhaps a glistening shower of pixie dust was falling outside. Perhaps it was the one evening in the whole of my life when I looked exactly like John Lennon.

I found myself playing doubles table tennis with Isobel Elliot, Evelyn Johnstone and Rae Smith, all in the year above me at the High School. There was a lot of colliding going on and no certainty about the score. At some unseen signal and with no hint of any prelude, Rae checked that we were the only ones in the youth club before closing the games room door and switching off the lights. In the pitch darkness I immediately discovered that all the agonising arithmetic counted for nothing. Three pairs of girly hands went everywhere while I tried hard to remember what a 6 was. And French Kissing? I thought I'd need dental work. I had no idea who was doing what to whom or how long this amazing event lasted, except that it didn't last long enough. But what dawned on me a moment before we heard the outside door squeak open was that not only did girls like sex, they wanted to put their hands inside your underpants to make sure you liked it too.

'Who's that?' whispered Rae. We frantically readjusted what we could find in the dark and although we were covered up when the Rev. M.A. MacLeod switched on the lights, there was little doubt that we had not been playing table tennis for a while.

Rae groaned. Her Dad was a member of the Kirk Session and an elder who often officiated on Sunday mornings. Isobel stood behind me while Evelyn Johnstone held on to the waistband of her jeans and smiled nervously. The minister flushed red, turned on his heel without uttering a word and stamped noisily out of the crypt. I discovered half an hour later where he had gone while Isobel was complaining about the ladder in her stockings and I was still a bit puffed. Having gathered all his Gaelic wrath about him, MacLeod had stormed along Inch Road to speak to my Dad. In front of Bina (Ma was on late shift at the Poorhouse) he described my wanton and disgraceful behaviour, adding that I could no longer expect to remain a member of the youth club and I would certainly not be going on next summer's church trip to Spittal Beach. They waited until the minister had ranted to a standstill, and then my Dad threw him out.

When I got home, still astounded by the orgy in the crypt, my Dad told me what had happened. I braced myself for the storm, but to my astonishment he did not give me a roasting, nor ask a single question or utter a note of criticism.

'Bloody hypocrite.' His own anger was warming up. 'Did he think I was going to listen to that and agree with him?' Why not Dad? You usually did. 'And where did he get that red nose and brosey face? Middlemas's lemonade? Bloody hypocrite.' He was up out of his chair now. 'And in my own house! That article came into my house to go on about one of mine.' He trailed off into the kitchenette where Bina was making a restorative cup of tea. 'Bloody cheek, Ma. Who does he think he is?'

I listened open-mouthed. I was used to weekly, sometimes daily bollockings from my Dad and had listened to him talk disparagingly about me outside my bedroom window. But here was something quite singular. A powerful local figure had mounted a pointed attack on his son, but instead of turning it back on me he had told the minister to get out of his house, repeating over and over to his face what a hypocrite he was. I couldn't understand it.

The day after the orgy in the crypt and its bewildering aftermath I met Rae Smith in the corridor and stopped to chat. With her nose in the air and fixing a thousand-yard stare she pushed past me and disappeared into the girls' toilets. Almost twenty years later I ran into her in Princes Street in Edinburgh. Same reaction, still not talking to me.

Smoking caused a lot less trouble. Unlike sex everybody tried it and most people did it regularly. Post-war British smoking culture appeared to be overwhelmingly naval; bearded sailors were to be found on packets of Players, heroes on Nelsons, gold stripes on Admiral and rigging on Weights. Cigarettes seemed somehow patriotic and drifts of blue-grey smoke wreathed almost every important domestic occasion in a homely, carcinogenic fog. Foreign fags were cool. When Alan Ladd flicked up a Lucky Strike out of one of those soft American packets where they tore a hole in the top, and lit up, he exhaled sophistication. And a Disque Bleu dangling on Jeanne Moreau's lip drew a man into those half-lidded eyes and transported an imagination to the cafés of the Left Bank and possible French Kissing. Even a tidy smoker like Omar Sharif could hint at undiscovered worlds when he tapped a black Balkan Sobranie on its box.

Frank Frost, Tobacconist, of Bridge Street, Kelso was a shop window on the world and it stocked all of these brands and scores more: oval-shaped Egyptian cigarettes, Philip Morris, Sweet Afton, Passing Clouds, yellow Gitanes, cork-tipped Nazionale and Carrol's Finest Virginia from Ireland. I tried them all, often sharing the expense with Pim Law, a very committed smoker from Yetholm and as much of a fantasist as myself. When we ordered black coffees in Lombardi's and lit a Gitane, we reckoned ourselves a pair of smiling, nodding men of the world. But only after we had picked the flakes of tobacco off our tongues and held back the tears and coughs when we inhaled.

Around the same time as I began to develop a taste for toasted tobacco I started talking. Talking, talking, talking, mostly trying out adjectives, comparatives, ideas, ambitions, trying things on for size. And talking, I suspect, mostly about myself and the tremendously interesting discoveries I was making in previously unexplored parts of my brain. James Clow seemed not to mind, and he listened uncomplainingly for years. From his posh house (Mr Clow owned a furniture shop) in Forestfield James walked down past Nana Hawkins' and round to 42 to call for me each schoolday morning. As as soon as I was over the doorstep the chatter began.

What persuaded James to be so patient is difficult to work out. First in our class at almost everything, he was easily the brightest intellectual spark at school, but I suspect his shyness and good manners inhibited him a little in the rough and tumble. We became good friends and I spent a great deal of time in the basement of his comfortable house. After we had exhausted all that Waddingtons had to offer we invented our own board game, unoriginally dubbed Europoly, which recreated the international tensions and conflicts of two world wars and converted them into recreation. Sometimes the labyrinthine rules meant that the Germans won.

James Clow's basement was a rare thing, an indoor space where teenagers could be undisturbed by adults, with its own toilet in the corridor, heating, light, privacy and some comfy old rejects from the furniture shop. But we never took girls there and hardly ever talked about them. Perhaps that was the result of a growing sense of exclusion which I felt at the time. Probably because I talked incessantly, hogged such conversation as there was, I began to find myself marginalised from the clannish teenage social scene, not invited to parties, safely mocked as 'big-headed' by knots of giggling confidantes. The most blatant example of this took place at a party I wished I had not been invited to. It was held in Lombardi's Café and I was sitting with a group of girls and some boys, chatting and laughing. When I came back from the toilet to rejoin the circle I found my chair had been pushed out and the others bunched up tightly, sniggering in a huddle as I approached. Other similar incidents took place and I remember being angry, upset and puzzled. No doubt I did talk endlessly about myself, not allowing other voices much play and I probably bored my contemporaries often. But I still didn't (and still don't) understand why I was so cruelly ostracised. In a small town, this was important, for there was nowhere else for a young person to go.

Of course Bina thought I was too good for the lot of them, 'a big, bang-looking boy', but she had no consolation past an awkward cuddle. Retrospective rationalisation can be highly coloured and suspect, but I do clearly recall how I felt at that time and what I decided to do about it. And exactly where I was when I decided.

One evening Bina had asked me to take something up to Auntie Meg Robertson's in Inch Road. The quickest route took me through a shortcut next to Richard Allan's house and between the back gardens. On the way back I dawdled a bit, looking around at the sheds, trellises of sweet peas and rows of banked-up tatties, thinking about nothing in particular. Scuffing across a green corner of Inchmead Drive, I heard myself begin to repeat something inside my head.

'No, no. No. No. No.'

I refused to let them win, beat me down to be quiet. No. No. No. I would not allow other people to tell me how it was going to be in my life. What course and shape it would take, how big or small it would be, what I thought I could do, achieve, be – all of that was going to be my decision. My life belonged to me. I would decide. And the way to start deciding for myself was to stop coasting at school, being lazy with homework, relying constantly on what one teacher called 'a native wit'. Schoolwork was the first thing, rugby the second, and whatever I could think of after that. I'd become so good at things, so famous that girls who didn't know me would queue up to be allowed to go on a date with me to school dances or maybe even the pictures. By the time the torrent of angry thoughts had been comprehended I found myself outside 42, standing on the pavement under my bedroom window. And my Dad, I'd show him too.

SIX

Education

THE SUNDAY PAPERS was a much better job than the Store milk. Not only was it one day a week, you didn't have to get up so early on that day. On Sundays no-one wanted a knock on their door much before 8 a.m. at the earliest. The pay was less but the earnings greater since some customers regularly added a small tip to the cash they handed over for their *Sunday Express* or *Sunday Pictorial*. And it was highly educational.

On the way round my round it was possible to read the *News of the World*'s racy bits (did I really see a story under the headline 'Naked Hypnotist Arrested at Co-op Bacon Factory'? Perhaps I only wanted to), scan the shiny new colour supplements in *The Sunday Times* and the *Observer* and go through all the rugby results at the back of the *Sunday Post*. The first two papers came up on the night train from London to Berwick-Upon-Tweed and the latter down from Tayside, but it seemed to me that they actually originated on different planets. The *Sunday Post* was universally bought and read. Everyone, except Miss MacHarg at the Woodside Stud (*Sunday Telegraph*), took the *Sunday Post*. It was an extraordinary newspaper in the Sixties whose editorial policy, devised in Dundee by the staff of DC Thomson, appeared to be built on the bedrock of Scottish small-town values. Brilliantly targeted, it was an indispensable item supplying weekly reinforcement for a wide range of attitudes and interests.

Most men read the front and back of the paper: the news stories and a comprehensive coverage of Border rugby, specially editionised for the area and often including reports on second and even third team matches. In the middle of the *Post* the features played well to women, particularly older women like Bina: 'The Doc Replies' was consulted like a survival manual and his (or her?) cautious and qualified advice universally taken, 'The Hon Man' was impenetrable to me but regarded as a great laugh, while the editorials and other regular columns informed a sense of an imagined community of couthy, comfortable and complacent Scots who were all Jock Tamson's Bairns, whoever he was and they were. Most influential were the iconic cartoons in the Fun Section. The Broons were an extended family living in Glebe Street, located in a town like Kelso, but probably more like Forfar, Brechin or Arbroath. Beautifully drawn, Granpa, Pa, Ma, Hen, Daphne, Joe, the good-looking daughter, the specky swot, the twins and any other Broons were the epitome of decency, their weekly non-adventures almost a guide to a cheery life of pipe-smoking conformity. Oor Wullie sat on an upturned bucket grinning at the world, something which must have been extremely difficult since the sharp bottom rim would have dug through his dungarees and into his backside. With his friend Fat Bob and a kindly PC Murdoch, Wullie inhabited the same unchanging universe as the Broons, and probably lived in the next street.

As I delivered the *Sunday Post* to every address in northern Kelso except Miss MacHarg's, none of these details occurred to me. All that came off its pages was tedium, not even dislike, more a sense that it had too much or too little to do with me, apart from the rugby results. In the increasingly competitive Sunday newspaper market of the mid-Sixties, circulation became less than universal. Not only was the *Post*'s readership beginning to die off, younger people were beginning to find the cosmopolitan world of the colour supplement a great deal more attractive, Carnaby Street more interesting than Glebe Street, and Mary

Quant's fashions a lot more interesting to look at than Oor Wullie's bucket. And 'The Doc' had more to say about arthritis than contraception. As I shoved them through letterboxes in the 1960s Sunday newspapers were changing, some of them growing too fat to fit into a normal letterbox. And through them I gathered an entirely impressionistic sense that the world they reported was changing too.

Many of my customers paid for their papers at the door and some of them supplied even more education. At Inchmyre the old prefabs where I was born were cleared away to make room for a few streets of low-rise flats. In the relative privacy of inside landings I gained some insights into modern marriage. The front doors of the flats had a glass panel in the top half, the frosted sort often fitted to bathroom windows. Having rattled the doorknocker I could easily make out the blurred shape of whoever was approaching from the inside, particularly on sunny days. More than once my arrival interrupted the sort of thing hinted at in the pages of the *News of the World* after its reporters had made their excuses and left. Punctuated by giggles, shushing and more remote bass notes I sometimes saw an obviously female form emerge into the hallway and in the four or five steps to the door slip on a dressing gown.

As I handed over the *Sunday Post* and the *Sunday People* or whatever, sorted out the change in monosyllables, and stared at the doormat, I was embarrassed. And also fascinated. Under their hastily tied dressing gowns these women were certainly naked, halfway through doing it with their husbands (partners only appeared in cowboy films) and definitely qualified at that moment to supply crucial information to anxious teenage boys. I think some of them smiled at me, knowing I knew and was probably blushing as I handed over their papers. Every Sunday I fantasised that I would rattle a doorknocker at Inchmyre, see the shape of a woman through the frosted glass, she would open the door and pull me inside, purely for my education, you understand. This happened, oh, at least a thousand times.

At one address I found my visit less of an interruption and more of an event. Every Sunday morning Mrs McGillivray came to her door in the Inchmyre flats wearing an ensemble of diaphanous (usually pink) nylon nightwear. She had black pubic hair. And a husband who kept roaring through to her to get a move on and close the bloody door, woman. He wanted his paper. What Mrs McGillivray wanted was less clear. With Mr McGillivray eating his fried breakfast only a few feet away from where we stood, it couldn't realistically have been me (could it? How? Where? On the landing?), and probably wasn't him either. She never said anything much past a comment on the weather and please and thank you, and her face remained expressionless throughout the ritual. Not that I was spending much time looking at her face, for Mrs McGillivray was not bonny and decidedly on the plump side. I never understood what the point of the transaction was and after a time I got so used to the little tableau that her thicket of pubic hair became part of the scenery, a surprise only when it wasn't on display.

I knew all of this would be new to Bindie McCombie when I asked him to take over my Sunday paper round for two weeks. So I didn't tell him. But before he did it on his own Bindie came with me on a week night to see how the ragged and inaccurate notebook of who got what matched up to who actually got what, if I could remember it correctly. Arithmetic was never a strong point and I'm sure that the people who ran the paper shop believed I was embezzling their cash. The truth is that I could never keep accurate track of it and if anybody benefited it was probably Mrs McGillivray and the young married ladies who got more back in fumbled change than they gave me in payment.

Bindie's takeover of the round was prompted by something entirely new to me, a fortnight's holiday in distant parts without my parents. A school trip to the Highlands had been organised by the best and most influential teacher I ever had. Johnnie Goodall (not that anyone ever dared call him Johnnie to his face) was a classical scholar who taught Latin to grumbling children who needed an O-Grade pass to gain entrance to university. In the Sixties Latin was mandatory for what the Scottish Education Department called the Attestation of Fitness (for university) and even scientists and mathematicians were forced to conjugate irregular verbs, translate (learn by rote, more like) bits of Caesar's *De Bello Gallico* and wonder why tables were feminine.

I liked Latin, at least initially because my Dad thought it was useless. It spoke of history, something I had become intensely interested in, and it also described the power and spectacle of the Roman Empire, its marching legionaries, racing chariots and world domination. It played to a childish need for order, and the ranked disciplines and absolutes of war games, the rows of toy soldiers arranged by centurions, maniples, cavalry, auxiliaries and all the rest. And the imagery had already been given celluloid form in countless Hollywood epics when Stephen Boyd, Richard Burton, and even old Victor Mature had buckled on the great-looking armour shaped to their manly chests, put on their hats with the red brushes on top, swept up their red cloaks, driven their plumed horses and led the tramp, tramp, tramp of endless lines of stern-faced legionaries through the deserts of Judaea, into dark German forests or accompanied by fanfares in the colonnaded cardboard sets of ancient Rome itself. Apart from a few SPQRs chiselled on entablatures or cast on the standards carried by the men in leopardskins, there was no sign of Latin. Steve, Richard, Victor and John Wayne never said '*Vale*' when they rode off to fight the barbarian hordes. None of that mattered to me because Mr Goodall supplied the real key to all of these stories and many more that never made it to the screen. The real Roman Empire expressed itself in Latin and a few weeks after mastering *amo, amas, amat* I reckoned myself a distinctly superior being, someone who sat in the stalls at the Roxy and was able to see past all of that Hollywood fakery, knew the real story behind it. I was well on the way to becoming an intellectual.

An Englishman who graduated from Cambridge University, Mr Goodall, it was alleged, turned up for his job interview at

Kelso High School wearing a bowler hat and carrying a rolled umbrella. It seemed to me that he knew about everything, could play the piano better than the music teacher, could direct school plays, drive a motorbike, run the bridge club and teach Latin, Greek and Ancient History as well. Also a keen hill walker, Johnnie Goodall began to organise school trips in the holidays, and in 1964 Bindie McCombie took over my Sunday paper round to let me go the furthest distance I had ever travelled from Kelso. It proved a stunning revelation.

We caught the train. Kitted out in anoraks, what passed for walking boots and rucksacks, we hiked up to Kelso Station to board a connecting service to St Boswells where Sheelagh Drummond, Sandra Black and Kenny bloody Lowson would join the party. From there we chugged north. Changing trains at Edinburgh Waverley we travelled to Glasgow, seeming to approach the formless sprawl of the great conurbation underground. Kelso started where the farms and estates stopped but it was much more difficult to tell where cities began and ended and on the journey between Edinburgh and Glasgow we never lost sight of houses and other buildings. Already I'd travelled further from Kelso than ever before. Since the onward connection left very soon after we arrived, Mr Goodall advised us not to leave Queen Street Station. And then it seemed that we crossed a frontier into another country.

Only a few minutes out of the Glasgow suburbs the Highlands rose up to meet us. In our compartment chatter stilled as we gazed at the sunlit majesty of mountains and sea lochs, what seemed to be a huge and empty landscape rolling away to long horizons on either side. Stations at Tarbet, Ardlui, Crianlarich and Tyndrum signalled another language. When the line climbed up to the bleakness of Rannoch Moor and looked over towards the bulwark mountains by the entrance to Glencoe, I began to feel overwhelmed by an oppressive sense of the place even though I knew next to nothing about its history. There was unquestionably an atmosphere of loss and emptiness, like an invisible mist, and each of the many times I have driven through Glencoe since then, the same feelings always come in on me. Reaching the sea loch coast at Ballachulish, Onich and Corran, it seems as though we had to travel through a tunnel of sadness to find the light at the end of it.

Mr Goodall had told us we were to spend a week of our fortnight at Garramore Youth Hostel, between Arisaig and Morar. The atlas I had at home was such a small scale that neither place appeared in it, and all I knew was that they lay on the Atlantic coast. When the train left Fort William to travel west along Loch Eil and around the spectacular Glenfinnan Viaduct with Loch Sheil stretching far into the distance, it seemed as though the gloom of Rannoch Moor and Glencoe was far behind us. And the Morar Peninsula, first seen in westering sunshine, appeared to me then like an unfolding revelation, the most perfect landscape I had ever seen. The moorland and mountains tumbled gently into the green sea, breaking into rocky outcrops and islets and fringed by miles of glistening white sand. Out in the Atlantic west the islands were backlit against the sun: Muck, Eigg, Rhum and the southern tip of Skye.

When we finally climbed out of the train at Morar Station in the early evening, we had three or four miles to walk to the youth hostel. The single-track road itself was magical, winding around small bays and the shoulders of hillsides to open up vistas far out to the islands and the ocean beyond them. Compared to the homely geometry of the Borders landscape, where fields, hedges and shelter belts seemed to sit together in tidy harmony, this was a place of wild majesty where the elements ruled. Near the mouth of the River Morar the ribbed skeleton of a shipwreck had been washed up hard against where we walked. In my mind I can trace every step of the journey from the station to Garramore. Thinking back on it now, nearly forty years later and after a great deal of travel to several continents, that small peninsula in the western Highlands remains for me unquestionably the most beautiful place in the world.

Far away from the claustrophobic routines of Kelso and Kelso High School we seemed to get on well as a group with none of the pettinesses that could play so rough. Out in the wide West Highland world there seemed to be more important matters to contemplate than each other's foibles. A group of twelve or so was small enough to cohere and yet large enough to offer choices of walking partners and for nobody to be driven to distraction for long by listening to me go on and on about how beautiful this place was. Across the single-track road from the youth hostel stood the green-backed dunes of Camusdarroch Beach. It is a shallow bay of white sand between the horns of two low headlands and it is best approached along the banks of a trickling creek that runs into the ocean at one end of the beach. Many years later Bill Forsyth made Camusdarroch world famous when he located much of the action for his film *Local Hero* in this breathtaking landscape.

Jennifer Wilson and I held hands on a long sunset stroll along the white strand and did some coy kissing amongst the dunes. Both of us were sure that to be in love at Camusdarroch would be wonderful, but unsure whether or not it ought to be with each other. The idea fitted the place but the moment was hesitant. Jennifer was one of the first girls I had a conversation with, and even found it possible to lay aside for more than a moment my anxieties about sexual arithmetic when we talked.

'Don't be so juvenile!' she once snapped at me when I tried some awkward manoeuvre that showed I wasn't really listening. Juvenile – from *Iuvenis, iuvenis*, adjective meaning young, youthful. Oh. Right. But I *was* young. We both were.

'Can't we just go for a walk?'

OK. In fact walking and talking with Jennifer was good once I'd stopped looking for handy places to lie down and get on with the arithmetic. It was not only that she had a bigger vocabulary (her Dad was a teacher in Yetholm and they probably talked like that all the time) but she could also use it to telling, sometimes crushing effect. More than anything, Jennifer was much more mature than I was, and when I stopped trying to compete with her I found myself in the unaccustomed position of listening. If I couldn't be in love on Camusdarroch Beach then I could certainly learn something. It turned out to be this: Jennifer gave me an early lesson that there was no such thing as talking to women, just talking, talking to people no matter what their gender, and interestingly if possible.

Youth hostels used to have an odd policy. You had to be out by a certain time in the morning, and even if it was raining torrentially, you weren't allowed back in until the end of the afternoon. In the West Highlands this stricture could be harsh, condemning a party of hostellers to a squelching and miserable tramp across the mist-shrouded countryside before throwing themselves on the mercy of the warden by claiming that the rain was on for the day. When it poured at Garramore we played Botticelli. Johnnie Goodall taught us this excellent game which requires no accessories, not even a pen and paper. It centres around the process of working out the name of a famous person thought up by a member of the party. All they are bound to supply is an initial, such as B for Botticelli, and then to answer a maximum of twenty questions with a yes or no answer. If the information gradually compiled does not discover the identity of the person then the thinker-up of the name has won, and if it does then the interrogators have succeeded. Disarmingly simple in conception, highly educational and very difficult if the mystery name is well chosen, it absorbed us for many rainy hours. On long car journeys I play it still with my children.

After a week at Garramore we made our way north to Loch Duich and Ratagan Youth Hostel. There Johnnie Goodall had arranged to meet three of his impressive friends: Dr Theo Cadoux taught Ancient History at Edinburgh University, his brother did something grand and their companion was a Welsh lawyer exotically named Hywel apRobert. They were all obviously intellectuals. And fit as bears. While we all straggled behind, strung out in a ragged line on the path up yet another bloody mountain, these three whizzed up and down Scotland's geography like the Road Runner in a hurry. When we finally caught up on the long summit of Beinn Fhada, they sat down and tucked into a sandwich lunch washed down by thermoses of sweet tea. We forgot to bring anything and I remember Jennifer Wilson's maturity faltering a little when I asked her for a bit of her chocolate bar.

Somewhere on that long mountain Johnnie Goodall and I found ourselves walking with the wiry Dr Cadoux, and without any prior warning, my Latin teacher suggested that I should consider taking Dr Cadoux's course and go to Edinburgh University to read Ancient History. Read? What? This was what the polonecks on Bamber Gascoigne's *University Challenge* did: they read things. And that's what Johnnie Goodall was saying. I should read Ancient History at a university. Me? This was the first time that anyone had included my name in the same sentence as the word 'university'. It was true that my sister Barbara had gone to Edinburgh University (I didn't know she was reading something. What was it?) but then she had won a medal for being Dux of Kelso High School, the brainiest person in our bit of the Borders. My Dad said the nearest I'd get to Dux was on the River Tweed. But Johnnie Goodall was being serious and I realised that through the mist Dr Cadoux was actually talking to me about what O-Grades and Highers I would need. I clambered down the skiddy slopes of Beinn Fhada in a daze. Reading Ancient History? I'd better start reading. And stop reading the *News of the World*.

It rained a great deal that summer on Loch Duich and the warden of the youth hostel took regular pity on us. But he did suggest that we might like to attend the local church so that we were at least out from under his feet for a couple of hours on a Sunday morning. And so while Bindie McCombie was looking at Mrs McGillivray's assets and checking out what was going on at the Co-op Bacon Factory, I was trooping along the lochside road to Letterfearn Kirk to sing a few hymns. Great.

When we arrived outside what looked like a large corrugated tin shed, scores of local people seemed to materialise from nowhere, all of the men scrubbed and suited, all of the women wearing hats and overcoats. No-one bothered to read the notice-board outside and consequently we were perplexed to discover in the pews large black books with *Am Biobull* embossed on the front and smaller volumes entitled *Am Salmadair,* neither of them printed in a language any of us could pronounce, far less understand. Every Sunday Letterfearn Kirk held a Gaelic service, all of it in Gaelic, including the Bible readings and the Psalms. Surveying his rain-swollen congregation the old minister muttered a few lines of welcome in what might have been English before sitting down in his little pulpit. And then a remarkable thing happened. From the front pews a tall and rickety old man rose slowly and without music of any sort, he began to sing. Except it sounded nothing like any singing any of us had heard before. In a swooping sequence of nasal notes, some held for many seconds, the old man intoned what appeared to be a line of something and then the whole congregation (except us) sang it back to him in unison with some variations.

I listened and watched open-mouthed. This was the first time I had heard the Gaelic psalmody and it transfixed me. My chest seemed to reverberate with the bass notes and the raw, primitive power of the music lifted me out of a rainy Sunday morning to somewhere I couldn't comprehend. Here was the sound of an entirely other Scotland, almost as far from the Borders as it was possible to get, and even further from Glebe Street and Oor Wullie's bucket. Many years later I learned to speak Gaelic and came back often to the Highlands and Islands, but when I hear the lines of the Gaelic psalms hung with glittering grace notes, soaring and dipping like flocks of birds high in the sky, their mystery remains untouched and intact. And I think of a summer in the mountains of the West and the eternity of the mighty Atlantic.

*

In third year at Kelso High School I opted to do Greek with Johnnie Goodall and was consistently first in the class, since there was only me daft enough to do it. Once again I decided on Latin and Greek precisely because my Dad thought it all a great waste of time. 'Christ! Dead bloody languages. Who you going to speak to? Eh? Julius bloody Caesar?' Dr Theo Cadoux, on the other hand, reckoned I needed both subjects at Higher Grade if I wanted to read Ancient History.

'Have you the Lion's part written? Pray you, if it be, give it me, for I am slow of study.' My first public utterance as Snug the Joiner in *A Midsummer Night's Dream* was another consequence of my Dad's disapproval and Johnnie Goodall's interests. 'Bunch of bloody jessies, walking about, gesturing and roaring at each other. Bloody acting. Acting the goat more like.' My Dad was partly right for Quince the Carpenter's reply to Snug's nervous enquiry was 'You may do it extempore, for it is nothing but roaring'. But he was wrong about the value of live performance in front of an audience and the immense lessons it offers to young people. It was admittedly difficult to make a mess of a small part like Snug's and relatively easy to use it as a means of gaining some confidence, even while cowering behind Shakespeare's lines. In fact our production was such a success I wanted more lines, was envious of Ronald Barker because Bottom had so much to do.

However the truth is that Johnnie Goodall had cast the play very judiciously. Ronald already possessed enough native self-confidence, bombast and projection for three Bottoms, and he did very well. But I discovered that performing was not something character-flawed jessies needed to do, in fact it was good for you, and very good fun. I enjoyed entertaining people and wasn't so shy that I minded them looking at me when I spoke my (very small) part. Since I have spent my whole working life in show business of one sort or another, I suppose I should regard these initial steps as formative and spend some effort on working out exactly what it was that attracted me to performing. The problem is that all I can remember is enjoying doing it and enjoying having done it even more, if it had gone well. That's all. And a cheering side-effect was the feeling of being part of a company, part of a group joined together by a common purpose which was enriched and made successful by precisely the characteristics which had sometimes led to my exclusion. Confidence, even some conceit, was useful for performers, while the demure moderation and craven conformity admired by those who pushed my chair out of the circle at the party in Lombardi's Café were no use at all.

Because Johnnie Goodall approached the job of directing school plays with real professionalism, we all learned disciplines which have certainly not deserted me. Between read-through and rehearsal everyone had to have their lines off word-perfect and as we approached the week of dress rehearsal, we had to know our bits of business and our moves by heart. Johnnie took two texts of the play and unbound them into single pages which he then gummed on to A4 sheets in a loose-leaf binder. Around the pages he plotted each scene, its composition on stage, lighting cues, sound effects and music cues. As I watched him do this (Snug didn't have many cues to worry about) I must have unconsciously absorbed one of the most important maxims for anyone interested in working in show business: talent is what gets you in front of an audience but forethought, hard work and meticulous preparation is what makes a success out of it. Like most young people, and a former member of the Druids, I imagined that performers just turned up and did it.

'I think we have a hit on our hands!' Johnnie Goodall burst into the dressing room grinning all over his face after the first performance of *A Midsummer Night's Dream*. We had played to a full house, but that was because tickets were bought by everybody's parents (except my Dad) and a few others. What had sent Johnnie in to congratulate us was a conversation with some schools drama person or other who had been raving about the show, and also several approving comments from other teachers.

The whole run sold out and we even gloried in a glowing review in the Kelso *Chronicle*, although it didn't mention Snug the Joiner.

The Dream (theatrical slang was acquired in a matter of days) inspired Johnnie and his company of actors to embark on a programme of productions for the rest of my school career. In a challenging contrast (too challenging for me, I had no idea what was going on) to the Shakespeare comedy, we played *Electra*, the classical Greek tragedy by Sophocles. Perhaps Dr Theo Cadoux recommended it. Jennifer Wilson took the name part while my old smoking companion, Pim Law, played her boyfriend (I think he was her boyfriend). I was his pal, constantly on stage looking spare, with no lines at all until I persuaded Johnnie to give me some of Pim's. As the audience concentrated (possibly) on the endless and impenetrable dialogue between Jennifer and Pim, I managed to stifle a sneeze one night and avoid falling over my sword on another. The following season Ronald Barker was unavailable (having moved to Stornoway) and so I landed the plum part of Major Sergius Saranoff in George Bernard Shaw's *Arms and the Man*. This story I could understand and hugely enjoyed all the Ruritanian business with shakos, those tasselly little jackets worn falling off one shoulder, black riding boots and a crop to smack against them. To say nothing of a black wig and a handlebar moustache. I'm not entirely sure what the audience thought but I certainly fancied myself. The most pungent recollection I have of Sergius, Snug and all those exciting times is a cliché: the smell of the greasepaint. No. 9 and No. 6 and the thick white remover cream all start my heart racing, even now, and a way of life began for me when Snug roared at the crowd.

Perhaps part of the attraction of acting was experimental. With Shakespeare's, Shaw's and Sophocles' lines to animate them we could all assume the fleeting characters of other people in other places, jump out of the everyday routines of home and school and feel ourselves really transported to a wood near Athens, Thebes or the Balkans. Sometimes real places near at hand could work a similar magic. Like many Borderers we went on holiday to the North Sea coast, to a caravan park at Spittal, near Berwick-Upon-Tweed. Because we crossed the border into England and found ourselves in a thoroughly different cultural milieu that existed only twenty miles from Kelso, caravan holidays were exotic and atmospheric.

The site lay on a gentle hillside between the seaside village of Spittal and the main line from Edinburgh Waverley to London King's Cross. It looked east over the rooftops out to the endless horizon of the grey North Sea. As the trains hooted and thundered past, steam trailing under the blackened bridge, and distant ships ploughed up and down through the waves, it seemed that our caravan was parked at a crossroads, a place where the drama and despatch of travel was hourly evident.

We spent most of our time on the beach and the sea-front at Spittal, shoving pennies in the slots at Tony's Amusement Arcade and buying dripping cones of ice-cream. Behind the promenade were gritty grey tennis courts, crazy golf and a putting green where you could hire clubs with tattered, unwinding leather grips. In an uncertain version of English holiday architecture the walls, paths and small buildings had been harled with pebbledash and painted a sickly shade of salmon pink. Wooden benches sleeved into concrete upstands were placed at intervals along the front. By comparison it was a tiny, poorly provided place for a holiday, but its novelty, the beach and the ozone sea air were such that we loved Spittal and as children went often.

After an ennervating afternoon on the beach with buckets, spades, crumbling castles and collapsing canals, we usually went back to the caravan to clean up before going out for fish and chips. One evening some time in the mid-1960s has always stayed with me. Climbing back up the steps to the park with the remains of my soggy supper in my hand, I heard my Dad say 'Will you just look at that.' I stopped and turned to see what he saw. Out over the sea huge clouds had darkened blue-black, and far to the east they clashed in a tremendous storm. Forked lightning crackled down to the surface of the water and lit the blackness in flashes. Thunder boomed in ear-splitting detonations and the sky grew darker and darker. Where we stood at the top of the steps an evening sun still shone, and behind us in the caravan park many people had come out to watch the heavens rage and some, like me, were transfixed, terrified by the immense, elemental power of the storm. Hidden in the cutting at the top of the hill behind us a racing express train bound for King's Cross rumbled and hooted, steam billowing into the summer air.

SEVEN

Departure

BY THE MID-1960s I had lost all interest in talking to Bina or listening to her stories, for a simple and predictable reason. As a restless, fidgeting, contradictory teenager I wanted to be somebody else somewhere else. Alistair Moffat's existence was boring, handknitted, homemade, small-time, small-town, the grey antithesis of John Lennon's, even Cliff Michelmore's. As Bina read her way through the *Weekly News*, smiling at Andrew Glen's adventures with his Border collie, Black Bob, I looked at the pictures and scanned the charts in the *New Musical Express*. My name didn't appear anywhere.

How could it? I was stuck in a rut, lived in a dump and every week delivered two hundred copies of the *Sunday Post* to nearly every house in our council estate, including ours. I couldn't even begin to imagine what Cathy MacGowan, Keith Fordyce or Simon Dee were doing on a Sunday morning, except that they wouldn't be reading 'Oor Wullie' or 'The Doc Replies'. Whatever it was they were actually doing, I wanted to do it too. All my thoughts (and particularly my plans for Sophia Loren) were predicated on escape from Kelso, and they amounted to a wholesale, brutal, thoughtless, heartless, careless rejection of everything Bina, and especially my Dad, represented. As usual my Ma seemed to understand very well what was going on, and she took the sensible course of making little or no comment (except once when I affected an interesting new accent, 'Not everything becomes you, Al'), letting me get it all out of my system, whatever it was.

As usual my Dad was ambivalent about his children leaving home, doing anything remotely risky, getting above themselves (or rather himself). Even though his promising school career had been cut short when he was forced to leave at fourteen, he resisted the proposal that my older sister, Barbara, should stay on at the school and try for university. Her exam results were excellent and my Mum's determination and pressure from Sandy Russell, the terrifying rector of the High School, finally swayed him. But each time there was a row, my Dad never failed to threaten Barbara with a dead-end job working in the clatter of the textile mills. When she won the Dux Medal I remember watching my Ma and Dad sheepishly, awkwardly walk on stage at the school prize-giving and thinking that he had a cheek turning up after all he had said.

And yet in his terms he certainly deserved to be there to bask in Barbara's achievement because he and my Ma had made the sacrifice of allowing her to stay on at the school. It wasn't that it cost my Dad anything, it was more that he had lost a proportion of any wages Barbara might have brought into the house if she had gone out to work at fourteen. A complicated set of expectations and obligations appeared to govern his attitudes, some of them inherited from Bina, and the mystery that was her family, her parents, her upbringing. It ran like this: in return for your parents raising you properly and supplying fourteen or fifteen years of free board and lodging, there was an expectation that somehow you would pay them back something before marriage arrived to confer a separate set of obligations. And at the end of your parents' lives, after age or infirmity had forced them to give up work and the ability to support themselves, it was expected that the balance of the debt would be repaid by caring for your parents until they died. Then everyone was released. It didn't matter that after 1945 the Welfare State had been set up to take over much of this because that was very recent history and these attitudes were ingrained, particularly in country families. In 1952 my Dad did not hesitate to bring my Gran to live at 42 Inchmead Drive, even though there was not the room, because he felt a powerful obligation to look after her in her old age. She had a state pension and the rent of a cheap council house at Hillbank Terrace, but all of that was overridden by the duty he felt, and when her initial objections had been overcome, was something that Bina herself ultimately understood.

When Barbara stayed on at the school, and then moved away to university for the first term, my Dad was heartbroken, wept in the car on the way back to Kelso after delivering his firstborn child to stay in digs in Edinburgh, giving her up into the hands of strangers. When he saw her wave goodbye at the window and bite her lip to stop a tear, it was all my Ma could do to stop him getting out of the car to take her back home. And at the slightest prompting, a less than happy letter home, or anything else at all, he wanted to go and get her 'right away, right this bloody minute, woman!' It wasn't just a mixture of anxiety and love, but a sense that the old bonds were sundering, the family he had made breaking up, the anonymous ghosts of his and his mother's past looking over his shoulder, whispering to him. And Bina always looking out of the living room window and down the road into the far distance. In his mind he knew that the destitution faced by farm workers too old to pick up a hoe did not await him, that the pension would pay for his needs after he stopped working and that his house would not be taken away. But in his heart he felt himself drifting, cut loose from the old women who raised him, the anchors of unarticulated and unconditional love that had held him fast all his life. He raged against the fact that he could do nothing more for his daughter, and that she could not reciprocate and was unlikely to at any point in the future. She was alone and with strangers, beyond his knowledge, control and help.

When my Dad turned to look at me, he shook his head, in constant despair at my contrariness, at how obvious it was that I longed to be away from him. But it turned out to be much easier for me. The knots of anger and frustration at Barbara's departure had slackened when my turn came. At the point when a decision was required, the arrival of the school-leaving age, there was scarcely a discussion. I just kept turning up. My Dad never knew exactly what subjects I took at O-Grade, except that they were mostly no bloody use to anybody, like Latin and Greek. When we actually managed to have a conversation of any duration about my future, it became clear, between the sighs and head-shakes, that he expected me to become a teacher.

'What the hell else can you do with bloody Latin?'

While he fiddled about irritably with his pipe I made a few alternative suggestions, and then in what I thought was some sort of conciliatory gesture, I asked him what he thought about it all. The explosion was instant.

'Christ! What the bloody hell do I know? Somebody as stupid as me? Eh! What have I got to give you that's any use? Bugger all!'

That was it. We never talked again about school, university, a job, or indeed anything much except rugby. When we could talk about nothing without arguing, we could always talk about rugby. We even argued about that, but since he knew a great deal about it, my Dad was almost always right and showed consistently good judgement about players, teams and games. And I had enough common sense to agree with him.

Perhaps as a result of our being able to talk about it, and also because I enjoyed the game, even seemed to have some natural ability, I began to take rugby much more seriously.

Inchmead Drive borders Poynder Park, the home of Kelso Rugby Football Club and ultimate destination for many French Letters posted under the grandstand. The ground was famous for other things, and most spectacularly for the first set of floodlights to be installed at a Scottish club. Switched on in 1961, they immediately attracted big games and big names to Kelso, and when their glow spilled into our street on match nights and the

to play in the Kelso High School First Year XV. Scotland had capped a sequence of heroic full backs: the impossibly named K.J.F. Scotland, C.F. Blaikie and S.W. Wilson, and I wanted to be like them. I particularly admired S.W. Wilson of London Scottish's brushed back haircut. Although I could catch, pass and kick reasonably well, I was going through one of my cylindrical phases and Bert Smith agreed to my choice with reluctance, perhaps thinking that my Dad had suggested this. The first match did not go well. Our forwards took a hammering and we never seemed to have the ball long enough for me to manufacture an explosive midfield intrusion and score a glorious try under the posts to seal the contest. Which was a pity because my internal commentary, by Bill McLaren out of Norman Mair of the *Scotsman*, had started well when I gathered the opposition kick-off and returned it with interest to the touchline. Good for the young Scotland full back, at twelve years old certainly the youngest ever to represent his country in the Five Nations Championship, to make a safe catch with his first touch of the ball. But as the opposition lineout jumpers leaped like salmon and many explosive breaks were detonated in the midfield with the Gala Academy backs running straight at me, it was clear that we were in for a hiding to nothing. The script for my glorious match-winning commentary was torn up and replaced by one which talked of heroism in adversity. My Dad talked about the score. 'Christ almighty! I heard you were lucky to get nil.'

In the early 1960s tradesmen were still working a five-and-a-half-day week and he had been spared the sight of our Saturday morning stuffing by Gala, but, as ever, he had been told all about it. Bert Smith took another look at my generous build and drafted me into the forwards. It was one of the few decisions taken by other people which radically changed my life. Unquestionably determinant. I believe that if I had been allowed to stay on in the backs I would have enjoyed my rugby even more and almost certainly have done more with it. It was only later I realised Bert's mistake. When I played senior rugby for Kelso, I

could handle, tackle and run as fast as those mostly useless arti-
cles who played in the threequarter line, but by then the die had
been cast and it was all too late.

Part of the reason why I didn't object louder and sooner was
that I enjoyed some success as a forward, and in 1966 I was
chosen to play against the under-sixteens Welsh Schools team.
They were huge, an immensely talented side with future Wales
and British Lions players having their first taste of international
rugby. At the lunch before the match, they were awarded caps
(with tassels), red blazers and ties, everything that the senior
players were given. We got a tie. And by contrast we were a
bunch of obvious kids, all shapes and sizes, one or two pairs of
dubious white shorts and a definite shortage of confidence. But
in the event we should have beaten them.

After our captain had told us to tackle, get up and tackle again
(should this have told me something? Would we ever have the
ball and make them tackle us?) and we had all shaken hands with
each other in a little ritual that may have come from the Famous
Five, I sat down in the corner to open what my Dad had given
me.

Before I travelled to the game my Dad gave me a Basildon
Bond envelope with my name on the front and told me not to
open it before I had pulled on the blue jersey, but to put it at the
top of my kitbag so I'd remember. It was the only letter I ever
had from him and the only emotionally calculated thing he ever
did. Sitting in the corner of the dressing room in the bonny blue
with No. 4 on my back, more nervous than I had ever been in
my life, I opened it. In the middle of the page he had printed
one sentence in capital letters. It said, 'REMEMBER WHERE
YOU COME FROM'.

It worked. I ran until my lungs felt like bursting, I tackled
every Welshman who came near me, sometimes when they
didn't have the ball, and when it was all over I was utterly
exhausted, every limb quivering. And yet it seemed all to be over
in a flash. About a minute after the referee blew his whistle to

start the game, he was blowing it to end it. We lost 6:3. I remember only one specific incident in what was a dirty game with plenty of sly punches and what Bill McLaren would have called 'fancy footwork'. The Welsh No. 8, a boy called John Bevan who later played for Wales and the British Lions, picked up the ball on his own tryline and galloped 70 yards down the pitch. I raced after him, and when he was forced to pass inside to his captain, Huw Jones, I wrapped him up in a tackle and dragged him down, preventing a certain score. And when Jones hit the deck I hit him as hard as I could, catching him on the lips and nose. Rarely has a punch been more richly deserved, for Jones was not a model of fair play or gentlemanly conduct.

None of this sort of thuggery found its way on to the back pages of the *Sunday Post*. When 'Fly Half' commented on the game, he was complimentary about the Welsh boys' performance, correctly picking out Bevan as a future prospect, but he did nominate Kenny Mallen of Gala and myself as the outstanding forwards in our team. On Sunday morning I folded each copy of the *Sunday Post* so that the match report was face up when I shoved it through the letterboxes. As usual Mrs McGillivray had nothing to say, and neither did I.

A year later a visit to the Maharishi and a fondness for long white shirts and Yoko Ono, or somebody, ensured that John Lennon had been jettisoned in favour of the much more heroic John Newcombe. The Wimbledon champion was so good-looking, played a macho serve-and-volley game hit with a satisfying whack, and smiled so much that there must have been a queue of women waiting outside, well, outside Wimbledon. No-one was waiting outside the public tennis courts at Shedden Park, but it was only a matter of time and a little serious practice. I was serving with the right sort of whack but was unable to keep the ball in Scotland, never mind the court. Racing up to the net after a serve was going OK but volleying was somewhat approximate. Down at the other end James Clow was being very patient, not having much to do when I was serving and smirking a few experimental Newcombe smiles as I bounced the ball menacingly on the baseline. Such as it was, my concentration snapped when I heard my name being called. Far away, walking across the cricket square, waving at me was Geoff Stevenson, the chairman of the Kelso selection committee, not for the school, not the Third XV, not the Second XV, but for the First XV, the senior team, entirely composed of men, some of them heroes.

'Right son.'

What, me?

'You're in the side for Edinburgh Wanderers.'

I dropped my tennis racquet.

'Murrayfield, tonight, kick-off at Six o'clock. Better get a move on.'

I dropped my jaw. Murrayfield? The same Murrayfield where Scotland play?

'I'll need to ask my Dad.' What? Why did I say that? I was seventeen and sure this was some sort of mix up, wind up. It was a fantasy come true, but I couldn't, didn't want to believe it was true.

'I've seen your Dad, that's fine. If you're good enough, you're old enough.'

I couldn't get my legs to work and was seized with several urgent needs.

'My Grannie hasn't washed my kit yet.' What? Any pin to burst the bubble.

'It's in the bloody car. C'mon.'

In the dressing room, on the same benches that France, Ireland, Wales, England, South Africa and New Zealand players sat on before internationals, I was sitting, still seized with some urgent needs. Wearing the black and white of Kelso, a red No. 1 on my back, I nearly burst into tears. Next to me was Jimmy Riddell, a giant of a man who would be pushing behind me in the scrum, second row to my front row. 'Stick with me son and you'll be fine.'

Our captain was a Scottish internationalist, a farmer never

anxious to use two words when one would do. 'Right lads,' the dressing room hushed for the team talk, 'Remember.' What? Remember what? 'This is a city team.' Not difficult, we are in bloody Edinburgh. 'A city team. Just a bunch of solicitors, accountants and poofs.'

'Poofs, Charlie?'

'Aye, poofs. I saw one of them come into the dressing room with his raincoat tied at the front.'

The poofs beat us 16 points to 5. Edinburgh Wanderers were Scottish club champions at the time. I was devastated and some-how felt it was my fault, no experience. Perhaps my Dad was right, just a shit, a shit in a bottle. But in the *Scotsman* the great Norman Mair picked me out as a promising player, and with Wattie Blake, the best in the Kelso pack.

'Well, just shows what he knows,' said my Dad on the evening after the game. He hadn't been in Edinburgh to see me play. How could he have any idea? I never understood that. He was desperate for me to do well at rugby, but equally desperate that in a small town, where everybody had something to say about everybody else's business, I shouldn't get above myself, shouldn't become big-headed. It was a disastrous miscalculation. Even though everything indicated otherwise, I thought myself no better than an average player, occasionally able to rise above the ruck. And when I went to university in London, I gave up playing rugby when it became expensive and difficult to manage without having a car. I don't entirely blame my Dad – other people did encourage me, and it was after all my decision – but I do bitterly regret stopping playing. I had a natural ability, not learned but innate I think, and it is close to a crime to ignore such gifts as we are given.

Perhaps these ancient regrets sound familiar, the pinings of a middle-aged wanna-have-been, meditations on possibilities that in reality were no more than that. But I don't think so. It was undoubtedly a missed opportunity and almost the only real sadness I have about wrong directions taken in the past.

The real past, that is, as opposed to the fantasy past. Such was my dissatisfaction with myself and almost everything around me and my certainty that almost anything would be better, I began to live a different life. Mostly this stayed inside my head, but when it did spill out, the effects could be bum-clenchingly embarrassing. In Berwick-Upon-Tweed with the long-suffering James Clow and Jock Boyd, we met some likely girls on the riverside walk. But instead of chatting them up in English, I had, for reasons that astonished my pals, and me, to do it in French, and pretend that I was a Frenchman who somehow came from Kelso, and had picked up no English, despite the irritating persistence of James and Jock in speaking to me in a language *je ne pouvais pas comprendre*. Perhaps I imagined that I was creating an easier cultural context for the later introduction of the subject of French Letters. None of these bemused lasses understood a syllable as I rolled my r's and nattered on about Bob Dylan in what I imagined sounded like Sacha Distel at his most irresistible, but they could recognise an idiot when they saw one. Looking at each other in a mood of *je ne sais quoi*, they turned and legged it up the stone steps to sanity and Berwick Bridge. James and Jock shook their heads and suggested we get some ice-cream. I spent the rest of the afternoon whispering an occasional remark, constantly looking around to make sure that the three lasses were nowhere in earshot in case they realised that, in fact, I was not actually a Frenchman after all.

Some fantasies grew like oaks from acorns, so fertile and willing was the ground. When my uncle Davie took to his bed with what turned out to be a terminal illness, I used to go along and visit him. The Browns lived only a few doors away in Inchmead Drive. My Ma's older and feistier sister, Auntie Isa, sometimes made tea and brought up a biscuit. One afternoon when the conversation lulled her into indiscretion, Isa began to answer some of my questions about my Gran and my Dad's upbringing. Lying on a bank of pillows, Davie was listening closely and after a moment or two he raised his hand to stop Isa in her narrative tracks. I think he was watching my face and realised that I knew nothing about any of this, and that it was not their place to tell me. Then Isa realised the same and began on a procession of diverting generalities about how lots of people moved around years ago, looking for work.

In the newspaper I had recently read a piece about travelling tailors and tailoresses, and we talked for a bit about how good my Gran was with her hands. But the article had said that many of these travellers were originally Jewish, and some suppressed their beliefs and identities, or abandoned them so that they fitted into whichever community they had adopted. My Gran's past was such a blank that it all seemed to fit. I put it to Isa and Davie that she might have been Jewish, might have come from the city originally.

'Aye,' said Isa with some relief at being able to cover her tracks, 'she might well have been.' Bina was short for Robina and it sounded like a Jewish surname. Maybe it was originally spelt 'Reubena'.

I took Davie's smile and Isa's nodding as agreement rather than the admission of a possibility they knew fine well was rubbish. But such was Isa's kindly unwillingness to upset me, Bina or my Dad, and Davie's tact about small-town mores that they simply let it stand. They didn't bargain for my prodigious ability to bark up wrong trees. The notion took root and grew in my mind, and for years I imagined that that was what made me different. I was obviously Jewish. That explained everything, my boy.

Janet was very obviously Scottish. The daughter of an Ettrick shepherd, the owner of a rich Borders accent and a heather-loup walking style that must have been passed on through her genes, Janet Elliot was in no doubt where she came from. Never gave it a second thought. And as such was the last person a Gitanes smoking, proto-French Jewish intellectual was ever likely to fall for. But I did, not kicking or screaming, fall head over heels in love with Bonnie Janet. Nothing could help me, she was so beautiful and gauche, her voice always on the edge of laughter, her directness so disarming, her openness like a summer breeze.

We were at a residential pre-university school at Carberry Tower near Musselburgh. Owned by the Church of Scotland and run by people in cardigans who seemed to smile all the time, it was an old country house temporarily taken over by Edinburgh University and opened to sixth formers allegedly interested in taking a degree there. About sixty young people arrived for what turned out to be a taste of university in more ways than the organisers organised. After supper on the first evening I decided to go out for a wander in the policies for some late sun and a good look around. Others did the same but for some reason I avoided the groups and pairings to find somewhere to be by myself. The grounds around the old house had been planted centuries before with single hardwood trees now in their splendid maturity, and on the edge of the parkland, by an iron-railed fence, I could see a chestnut whose tresses touched the grass. It was cool and dapple-shaded under the green canopy, and I settled on the knotted bole for a quiet cigarette.

'Got one spare?' Janet must have followed me across the park. 'Yugh! French fags. Yugh!'

She threw it away amongst the twigs and immediately jumped up to stamp it out. There had been no introductions, only a shared interest in smoking, and chestnut trees with privacy.

'Where you going?'

'St Andrews.'

'Oh, me too. Just came on this for a laugh.'

Something made me keep quiet – normally I would have been halfway through the second half against Edinburgh Wanderers by this time, having dived off to the touchline for a discussion of the new Dylan LP, or Ted Hughes, or Thom Gunn. In retrospect I realise that Janet had the initiative and she would decide who said what, or did what, next.

'I know who you are. I'm Janet Elliot, from Selkirk.' And then she kissed me.

I thought, 'Christ! She fancies me, she did it first, and I fancy her!' Janet was big on lipstick and before we could step out into the sunshine there was a lot of hanky dabbing and fixing. Impressively she had a compact case in the back pocket of her jeans, which were so tight that it was a business to extract it. 'Christ! She's gorgeous, and she fancies me. No question about it. Bloody hell.'

The summer of 1968 was magical, almost dream-like. But I hardly noticed the student uprising in Paris, Daniel Cohn-Bendit or Rudi Deutschke. For me the famous graffito, '*La Rêve, C'est la Réalité*' meant something quite different. I was in love with Bonnie Janet and I spent the summer in her brother's car as she drove us to parties, Young Farmers' barn dances and common ridings. It was a huge purple Vauxhall Zephyr with slidy leather seats and enough room in the back for passengers as well. I was working on the grain bins, and although we regularly put in twelve-hour days through the week, we always finished early on Fridays. If we were anywhere near, one of the guys could usually be persuaded to drop me in Selkirk. At 5 p.m. the hooter sounded at Ettrick and Yarrow Spinners, the gates opened and scores of women emerged. With her lipstick intact, smudges on her chin and cheeks from the oily machines and her hair everywhere, Janet looked sexier than a hundred Brigitte Bardots. And when we cuddled and kissed arm in arm up the steps to the town, she smelt of sweat and cigarettes. I adored her. Her workmates chaffed Janet at the muckle big man waiting at the gate to meet her, and she leaned round me to give as good as she got. There was no doubt that Janet was running this and in the women's world of the mills, I found myself the one who said little and did most of the smiling.

How she planned our weekends I have no idea, but as soon as Janet was through the door at Kirk Wynd, she went into dressing-table overdrive. Her mother, Ella, worked in the Cottage Hospital, often on night shifts, but she seemed unconcerned, made no enquiries and put my stuff in the back bedroom. To save time I used Janet's bathwater, but I was always ready ages before her. Ella's baking tamed the pangs and we sat happily in the front room until the grand entrance. 'You ready?' Janet bounced through the door in whatever creation had been planned all week, and with a peck on the cheek and a hunk of Dundee cake from her Ma, we were into the Vauxhall Zephyr and off.

At Harmony Bird's barn dance at a farm near Jedburgh Janet knew everyone and I knew nobody, as usual. But that was fine since the dancing was in lines and squares, and the band had a caller to guide the ignorant, like me. Drink driving had not yet been invented and after the dance Janet happily drove back to Kirk Wynd. I wasn't sure but I didn't think I would have to do anything. We cleaned our teeth and kissed goodnight on the landing.

Moments later I heard my bedroom door creak. 'You asleep?' whispered the shape against the streetlit window, 'Course you're not.' And she slid in beside me with a kiss and put her head against my shoulder. I loved her.

EIGHT

Remembering the Days

EVEN THOUGH IT was June, Bina had made stovies with a tin of Fray Bentos corned beef chopped into them and plenty of lard.

'Now. Whatever you've been doing, I don't want to know.' A sentence which seemed to have been maturing for a while in Gran's head as she looked out of the living room window and down Inchmead Drive. When my Dad drew up at the kerbside, bringing me back to Kelso from my first year at St Andrews University, I waved at Bina, but she didn't bother with such nancy trivialities and was pulling herself up out of her chair to get away into the kitchenette and get the stovies on. God knows what sort of bloody rubbish they fed them at the university, that's if they bothered to eat anything at all. Drink, more like.

'Help my God, will you look at the state of these!' Bina was going through the plastic bags full of dirty washing and had found several pairs of miniature woollen socks. Before I first left for St Andrews ('there'll be a right lazy wind off the sea there. It'll go through you instead of round you') she had knitted for weeks to produce industrial quantities of warm socks, but machine washes at the laundrette in Market Street had shrunk them to baby sizes. I enjoyed her rows and admonitions as much she did, and the sighs of half-hearted exasperation carried inside them a secret language of love. And we both knew it. Watching the old woman shuffle around the kitchenette in her slippers, shaking her head and tut-tutting at everything I said about university, I realised how much I had missed her fussing concern about what was important in life, like stovies and warm socks, the things only she could do for me. But after the longest time apart, nearly a year with one or two breaks, I could see a change in Bina. She was beginning to founder, suddenly much older and slower than she was. When I tried a kiss and a cuddle ('Here! Stop that nonsense. Away you go!'), I felt the bones in her back, and the smell of oldness stronger than ever. Even her occasional spats with my Ma seemed half-hearted and in the weeks that followed Bina talked to me less than she used to, smiling and nodding at my stories rather than the usual who-do-you-think-you-are, not-everything-becomes-you, you know, remarks.

At the Easter vacation I'd been to see Auld Jim Wallace for a job. Agricultural Engineers and Millwrights, Wallace of Kelso had a thriving summer business erecting sheds for cattle courts or silage and tall grain bins for storing dried corn. On the Monday morning after coming home I reported for work to the foreman, Pouf Turnbull. He most certainly wasn't gay, and the origins of the nickname were so venerable that they had vanished from memory. Even so, it was a nickname few dared to use to his face. In the late 1960s there seemed to be plenty of work to report for because farmers were able to negotiate substantial subsidies to improve their steadings with new buildings and Wallace's won many contracts. Part of the reason for their success was Auld Jim's distinctive management style; overheads and confusion were kept to a minimum by an unwillingness to commit very much to paper and also an old-fashioned approach to industrial relations.

'What! Man, damn you. Just get on with it!' was Jim's standard response to most reports of problems no matter how difficult. And it worked. Rather than stand about grumbling that something would never work, most of Wallace's men just got on with it the best way they knew how. Doing anything was better than doing nothing. And in any case many of these tradesmen had an individual pride in their work, almost as a way of showing up, of spiting their bosses. And the phrase 'he never put bad work off his hands' signified the highest praise. A wee man who wore a cream linen jacket in the summer over a white shirt and tie and trousers with a waistband pulled up to just below his armpits, Jim Wallace was old enough to know that most problems would simply go away if left untouched, and those that wouldn't were just facts of life to be borne with fortitude.

The methods of pre-fabrication and construction of Wallace's farm sheds were straightforward enough. Girders for stanchions were cut in the workshop to a uniform length and roof trusses made to suit. Between each truss standard-sized wooden purlins were bolted on to cleats, and they stiffened the whole structure, pulling it together into true. Before the steel arrived at the farm, holes were dug for the stanchions, and it was this initial part of the job which caused most problems. To save money farmers often used their own diggers to excavate the holes without using a theodolite, or sometimes without even a line to keep them in a straight line. The result was that a shed erected in postholes of uneven distribution and depth would never stand square, and nothing – sheets of roofing asbestos, purlins – would fit properly unless the holes were dug out again, by us. But true to Auld Jim's maxim, we just bloody well got on with it and sorted out the problems as we came across them.

Tow Lauder led the squad in the summer of 1969. Not a big man but possessing a pair of immensely powerful hands (he could bend what he called 'ern' or iron rods in front of his chest like a circus strongman), he mixed hard work and fun in the right measures. Because we worked on bonus, the length of time taken to build the shed properly was all that mattered. I remember early starts driving into Berwickshire against the sunrise, when the cool was still on the morning, when Tow and his platoon of three were barely awake, having got home only seven or eight hours before. Crammed into the cab, I had to endure three enthusiastic smokers (I'd temporarily given up) and coughers.

Usually I hung out the window, occasionally dodging roadside vegetation.

Once on the site it was my job to unload the big drums of electrical cable and go off into the steading in search of power points. On dairy farm places we often got a drink of fresh chilled milk first thing. And no-one had heard of skimmed milk in those days. What cost Wallace's most cash and was absolutely critical was the crane. It was hired from Berwick-Upon-Tweed if we were down the valley and Galashiels if we were up, and a good job was one where we finished quickly with the cran-man. Using a long jib, he lifted the steel girders by chains I had attached a foot or two from the middle so that they would come up near to vertical. And then we placed the bottom end into the posthole, and once four were bolted together like table legs, we filled and packed the bottom with stones and concrete, hoping that high winds would not blow them off the straight overnight. Once that basic structure was up and right, the rest was much easier, with bays of stanchions and trusses added quickly and bolted together with purlins.

It could be a dangerous job, an undoubted fact that seemed to bother no-one. Tow and the others sometimes worked fifty feet off the ground, sitting on swaying trusses trying to get a secure bolt into a purlin to stiffen the thing. No-one used a safety harness (what could it be attached to – sky-hooks?) and even though we had a first aid kit, a few lint bandages or a strip of Elastoplast would not have made much difference to anything. If anyone had fallen they might have been killed, certainly badly hurt. But even when it was wet, the squad walked on the steel girders without a second thought, sometimes only gripping the inside edges with their toes through heavy boots. What could have happened if the crane had ever lost a girder or the first unstable structure had fallen doesn't bear thinking about. The truth is that we didn't even think about it. In those days no-one did and while no member of our squad ever did anything daft, legal notions of health and safety at work had yet to be set in place of everyday common sense. Since I was least experienced, and only a bloody student, still at the school, I was groundman, throwing up tools and bolts, attaching ropes to lift purlins, relaying shouted instructions to the cran-man, and once or twice, without a licence, driving to a phone box to place big Sandy's bets.

We ate a great deal. Fourteen- to sixteen-hour days of hard labour every day needed many calories to sustain that pace, and tiredness could be dangerous. Bina used to make me a big piece, perhaps six or seven sandwiches (usually Store cheddar and tomato on doorsteps of plain bread), an apple, chocolate biscuits and a thermos of milky tea. I can remember being so exhausted once that I was shaking, but ten minutes after bolting down some food, the tremor stopped and I felt OK. Chocolate worked fastest. Sometimes on a fine night when we were nearing the end of a big shed, the farmer might bring out a few tins of beer and some shortbread. I used to take a wander round at times like that and see how we had changed the landscape. What stays with me from that summer on the sheds is the memory of working in some beautiful farm places: Broadmeadows near Selkirk, Byrewalls in Berwickshire where I fell asleep in the hay barn and the bastards covered me up, West Allerdean in North Northumberland where the farmer had to say 'Cannot you get the bolt in the hole?' about six times before I understood him. And Barmoor where I fell off a roof and into some straw bales before rolling down them into a stinking pool of silage liquor. I sat in the back of the pickup on the way back.

Perhaps because I knew I would leave it all behind me soon, I looked often at the landscape of my childhood in those summers working at farm places. Sometimes when the job went well and quickly, the bonus was high and I had the weekend and my girl to look forward to, I imagined it as a wholesome sort of a life. The same rhythm of the lives of almost everyone I knew. 'Aye, maybe,' Tow Lauder was sceptical, 'you might say that now, but think about the winter, and the fact that you're not down to do this for the rest of your life. Wait till your hands are bent like claws and it's a business to get out your bed and over the door in the morning.' And he was right. No matter how the Cheviot Hills shimmered in the midday haze and how good the beer tasted after a week's hard work, it was in reality a life that I could never sustain or even fully understand.

'Did you get it at the weekend then?' At the breakfast break on a Monday morning none of them wasted much time on pre-liminaries. All of the others in the squad were married men, with only a sentimental interest in what young people got up to on a Friday and Saturday night with their girlfriends. Or didn't. My usual coy refusal to answer either way was always taken as a no.

Tow and the squad were also curious about university. 'So. The lassies. Do they?' Of course! I made up so many wild stories that after a day or two of orgies and aristocratic nympho-maniacs, they realised it was a mild retaliation for all that student prince stuff I'd had to suffer at piece-times or on the road back at the end of a day. 'How old are you now? Still at the bloody school? Must have been awful slow at the reading and writing.' Tow had an infectious laugh and could barely tell a story because the next thing he was about to say amused him so much.

The most attractive conversations, the quiet ones where I shut up and learned something, were with Doddie Pie Lillie. A slater to trade with R&W Charters, he was enormously well read, had an encyclopaedic knowledge of the Borders and was the only man of his generation to ask me detailed questions about what I actually studied at university.

Once on a roof at Doddington, on the edge of the Milfield Plain in North Northumberland, I was standing on the ridge looking north-west towards the setting sun. 'Aye,' Doddie Pie was climbing the sword ladder behind me, 'You see things up here that you'd never see, unless you knew what they were. This is when you get a right long look at the land.' He pointed out how the oblique evening light showed up the run-rig ridges of high-altitude medieval ploughing, the rings of ramparts on a hill fort, and once, the playing-card shape of a Roman camp.

But Doddie could also take the piss, literally. At one big estate farm we had finished a shed which sat close to the grand farmhouse, and when I complained I needed to pee but hadn't the time to climb down, he assured me that nobody was around to watch me piss off the roof. A sixty-foot stream splashed on to the cobbled steading just as the farmer's wife, seen of course by Doddie when he advised me to go ahead, rounded the far corner. I couldn't stop once I'd started, but she stopped, put her hands on her hips and watched me until I'd zipped up my jeans. Bastards.

Even though my Borders accent returned the moment I got in the car at St Andrews with my Dad, I was really at the beginning of the process of losing it, of leaving, and those valedictory summers working on the sheds and the grain bins and with Wallace of Kelso and R&W Charters were the last time I felt part of it, part of my childhood, indistinguishable from what English people call 'background'. The truth is that in my heart I didn't want to leave it, but as Doddie Pie pointed out, I had to. Nothing was surer.

Alison Renton knew it too. I met her at a Young Farmers dance at the Tait Hall in Kelso, and she immediately made a strong impression when she offered me a ride in her MGB GT. A red sports car of the kind you had to lie down in and crawl out of on your hands and knees, it made a satisfying snarling noise, and when Alison threw it round the blind corners of country roads, I felt I was undergoing some sort of test. And failing it, feeling more than slightly ill. I had read something in the James Bond books about how trips in fast cars would guarantee that women would sleep with you. Perhaps if I told Alison I would anyway, she might drive a bit more slowly, or even let me out to throw up. Like most of the children of Berwickshire farmers she was car-mad, and wore those driving gloves with holes and bits missing on the back, as well as sunglasses whatever the weather. Perhaps she had read the Bond books as well.

After the dance was over I went back to her parents' farm with a bunch of young farmers. Alison had invited us all for coffee (and promised to run me back to Kelso afterwards, it was no trouble, she liked to drive, honestly) and in the big farm kitchen she set about boiling the kettle, finding cups and biscuits. One of the snootier young farmers made a joke about the ancient biscuit and cake tins put on the table, and I realised I was keen on Alison when I leaned across and whispered to him that I'd shove them up his arse if he didn't mind his manners.

On the road back (I remember it crystal clearly, a light blue sky against an inky-black landscape, which whizzed past me at high speed) she told me that Edinburgh University was OK, but that it didn't seem to belong to anybody, certainly not her. It was a curious thing to say, a way of arriving at the notion that if no-one owned the place or the institution, at least emotionally, how could she come to care about it enough to let it pull her away from Berwickshire. And in any case she would only be there for four years at the most before moving on somewhere else, and then maybe somewhere else again. Despite the fact that everything of any interest to young people appeared to be happening in cities, Alison didn't want to be in Edinburgh, she loved the big skies of Berwickshire and was finding it hard to leave them behind, just as I was. In the event she never had to. A few months after we made that journey, my Dad told me that she had been killed in a car crash on the A1. It was a fatal cruelty I've never fully accepted, and although I only knew her for part of a summer, I often think about Alison and the little red car she died in.

What sharpened my own sense of leaving home was something more immediate than her musings about ownership. Despite the fact that the club had offered to pay my travelling expenses from St Andrews, I didn't come home every weekend to play rugby for Kelso. Not being able to drive (my Dad's attempts to teach me had almost ended in a fist fight – while I was driving the car along a busy road), I had to rely on inadequate and slow public transport. It took five hours to get from the East Neuk of Fife down to the Borders, and after 6 p.m. on a Saturday it was impossible to get back. And so I played for the university and not my home town.

During the summer of 1969 the work on the sheds had hard-ened up my flabby student muscles a good deal, and at the weekends I went down to the long beaches of the North Northumberland coast to learn how to sprint properly with a school of professional runners. We began each session with the sand dunes. Running at least ten repetitions up a dune when each pumping stride advanced only about six inches in the cas-cading sand was lung-bursting. When the tide went out, we ran on the damp and firming sand as I found out about knee-lift and arm action. One of the school wore sunglasses as he trained ('Sunglasses? They're not sunglasses, they're my re-entry shields'). When it came to fitness training for the new rugby season, I found I was ahead of most players. But pre-season sessions at Poynder Park were not what I expected. Now that I had left to go to university and hadn't turned out for Kelso recently, some established players felt that I shouldn't be considered for the pres-tigious sevens tournaments in September, even though I was available. Occasionally fists flew at training, and much more dan-gerous, when I jumped for the ball at a lineout, one of my so-called team-mates took the legs from me when was in the air. I landed on my shoulder and neck, only just avoiding serious injury. Another player tripped me with his feet as I went past him, and several regularly refused to pass me the ball even though I was running outside them in a try-scoring position. All of that added up to a great shame, and another clear signal that I had no choice but to become someone else, no longer a Kelso man, but a man who came from Kelso.

The following summer I worked at R&W Charters for a few weeks to raise enough cash to travel. Aside from the romance of the thing, the immediate spur to explore bits of Europe was a course organised by the Medieval History Department at St Andrews University. It was to take place at the British School in

Florence. All of us who had opted to do the Italian Renaissance course ('Italian bloody Renaissance! Christ allbloodymighty, will you ever learn anything useful?') were expected to attend, go to the galleries and learn some Italian. I decided to fly out to Istanbul, spend time travelling through Turkey ('What kind of a place is Torquay? Somewhere down in England?' asked Bina) and Greece, and arrive in Florence from the east. In the event I missed the connecting ferry from Patras in the Peloponnesus to Brindisi, saw it leaving the harbour as I got off the wrong bus. It was the S.S. *Hellenia* and a few hours later the ship sank with all hands. Back in Kelso my Ma was beside herself when she saw the news of the disaster on the television news. After some long days of uncertainty, the minister, Donald Gaddes, finally obtained confirmation from the British Consul in Naples that my name was not on the manifest.

Unaware of any of this, I had caught a later boat and was travelling to Florence in a bus, barrelling along the *autostradas* before alighting in the Piazza Santa Maria Novella in the cool of the early morning. I had two pressing problems. Some weeks before, I'd agreed to meet my great friend, Tommie Pow, at the British School at 55 Lungarno Guicciardini, wherever that was, at 1 p.m. on a date in September – which turned out to be a Sunday. The second pressing difficulty was nylon. Like most young men in 1970 I had long ago rejected flappy old cotton underpants for nylon versions – easy to wash, fashionably brief, strongly elasticated and very butch. I had purchased a pack prior to departure for Turkey. They were the source of sustained agony, chafing so badly in the heat against my tender, sweaty skin in a particularly sensitive place, that I was red raw when I got off the bus. Truly unforgettable. Walking like a cowboy with rickets, I carried my rucksack around a Florentine Sunday searching for 55 Lungarno Guicciardini. 'Loongarno? OK. Sorry, *scuzi*, I mean.' Taking a direct route through a blatter of pigeons in the Piazza della Signoria, I discovered the joys of the Loggia degli Lanzi – not the beautiful Donatello and Cellini sculpture, but the cool marble steps leading up to it. With no-one around to wonder what I was doing, I arranged my shorts in such a way as to reduce the fiery temperature for a few blissful moments. At 1 p.m. sharp I staggered into a doorway marked Scuola Something-or-other and walked up more wonderful stone steps, ice-cold they were, and reached the locked door of the British School of Florence, Principal, Ian Greenlees. No Tommie Pow, but punctuality (better never than late, I said, much later) was not a strength. When I heard a door open and some echoic clumping and cursing, at about 1.15 p.m. (these details were important), I eased myself to my feet and hid behind the lift in the stairwell until TP had gained the landing. And before he could begin to huff about me being late, I gave him the most earth-shattering fright I could manage.

'It's the very dab.' Tommie was offering several shakes of the Johnson's Baby talc his Mum had packed. In the Pensione Antica a sign above the bath announced '*Bagno Freddo Gratuito, Bagno Caldo L500*'. I guessed wrong and suffered the mixed pleasures of a hot bath, before giving way to my sweaty friend, 'Pity to waste 500 lire.' After buying loose-fitting cotton underpants: '*Pantalone di sotto.*' '*Scuzi?*' 'Eh, em, well, underpants.' '*Ah le mutande! Si, va bene,*' a large tin of talc, '*Ah. Si. Talco,*' and taking things one day at a time, I found myself miraculously restored. And ready for culture. That was why I had made my painful way across south-eastern Europe, culture. But nothing prepared me for what Florence was to show me.

I discovered a different world, a city and a people in love with beauty. As Tommie and I made our way to the Scuola on the first morning we passed beautiful buildings bathed in buttery light, beautiful sculpture in every public space, and to animate the city some of the most beautiful men and women I had ever seen. The Arisaig peninsula may be the best thing God made in western Europe, but Florence is surely man's greatest creation. We were taught Italian by Signor Donati: '*Coraggio, Signor Pow! Coraggio!*', and looked after by the lovely Leia and Federigo at the Pensione Antica in the Via de Pandolfini. When Chianti-fuelled exuberance reached too audible a level, Leia laughed and sent her battleaxe mother-in-law to rap for '*Silenzio!*' on our door.

As though we were filling up a space we never knew was empty, Tommie and I devoured Florence, saw everything at least once and marvelled daily at how the worship of beauty reached into every corner of the city. After several attempts, we gained entry to Santa Maria delle Carmine to see the fresco cycle in the Brancacci Chapel. Painted by Masaccio and Masolino ('Big Tom' and 'Wee Tom' announced Our Tom), it told the story of the Tribute Money and the Life of St Peter. The chapel is very small and we were the only people in the church. In the darkness of the nave, monks flitted about their business and left us to ourselves. Without saying very much past 'What a thing this is!' or 'Look. Will you look at that,' we allowed our eyes (actually there was no choice) to be drawn into the power of what Big Tom and Wee Tom had made more than 500 years before. The achievement of the thing moved me to head-shaking silence and TP to tears. We walked up and down the tiny chapel having lost all sense of time, looking, looking, looking. It was the first time I had been moved at all by a picture on a wall, although I had faked it a few times so as not to feel left out. And when we finally blinked out into the afternoon sun of the piazza, Tommie turned to me: 'No more today, that's me done.'

One of the many joys of having him there was the process of articulating to each other what we had seen in the Uffizi, the Pitti and elsewhere; saying what we thought helped to organise what we really thought. And there are memorable pleasures to be had in seeing beautiful things together and comparing, arguing and thinking aloud. But that day, after seeing the Brancacci Chapel for the first time, we went for a beer and talked about girls, I think.

Before supper at the Pensione Antica, it became our habit to watch *l'ore del passiagato*, literally, the time of the walk. There appeared to be a traditional circuit starting at the cafés of the Piazza della Signoria, moving down to the Arno, across the Ponte Vecchio and back again. Tommie and I positioned ourselves near the Cellini bust halfway across the Old Bridge (people seemed to stop, look down at the river and turn back) and, working our way through a pack of Nazionale, we gawped at the procession. The time of the walk was for seeing and being seen. Gaggles of olive-skinned girls with stunning white smiles and flawless figures passed as if in an endless stream, dressed to kill. It seemed not to matter that they were entirely unattainable, they were just very beautiful, walking in the warmth of the evening, and that was enough for us. Just to see them. In any case the boys looked so good that two bearded denim-wearers, slightly tanned, from pasty-faced Scozia were unlikely to be noticed.

Several other undergraduates from St Andrews University came to stay at the Pensione Antica but most seemed more interested in a holiday. But Iona Stevenson was so terrified of Italian men grabbing handfuls of her bum that for days she refused to leave the *pensione*, preferring to pine for her boyfriend from Dundee. When Tommie and I offered to escort her (TP's assurances that all the Italian girls were much better looking anyway, so she had nothing to worry about really, failed to do the trick for some reason) with me at the front and him at the back, walking along like Egyptian sand dancers, she was finally persuaded. Dressed in a fine cheesecloth skirt and shirt, with a silk scarf tied over her hair, looking great, Iona stepped into the lift after I had checked it out for bottom-pinchers. Once we ventured into the street, with Tom and me in position, we made it all the way to the corner of the Via de Pandolfini. And then a pigeon shat on Iona's head. First gasping at the shock of seeing green, slimy poo dribbling down her silk scarf and on to her forehead, we soon stuttered into hysteria as Iona screamed and fled back to the *pensione*. On our hands and knees on the pavement, barking with the pain of laughing so hard, we took days to recover. Iona never did.

Many years later, I took my Ma on a trip to Florence. After listening to me talk endlessly about my visit, what amounted to my

PART II

NINE

In the Winter's Room

MY HEADLAMPS COULD not penetrate the blizzard further than a few feet, and in fact their outshot beam seemed to make it thicker. The snowy windscreen flickered like interference on a faulty television. It was hypnotic, concentration-sapping. Through south Edinburgh I drove on sidelights, navigating between the lines of streetlamps. There was no-one else on the road, not even any buses. What kept me focused and drove back thoughts of my Dad was the near impossible business of driving. I crawled through Dalkeith and up the long hill out of the town. These were the last lines of streetlights and the blizzard blew harder as I gained height, plunging into the blackness of the freezing night.

To fill up all of the spaces in my head, I shoved a music tape into the player and turned the sound up full blast. It was impossible not to listen. Sixties hits pounded out their simple rhythms: 'California Girls', 'The House of the Rising Sun', 'The Mighty Quinn'. I remembered ordering *Sergeant Pepper's Lonely Hearts Club Band* in 1967 and persuading my Dad to give me the keys so that I could play it on the deck at the new rugby club hall. The speakers were huge, mounted on pillars, floor to ceiling. 'I heard the news today oh boy/Four thousand holes in Blackburn, Lancashire/And though the holes were rather small/ they had to count them all/Now they know how many holes it takes to fill the Albert Hall/I'd love to turn you on.'

An hour before, sitting at home in Edinburgh, I had jumped when the phone rang: 'Is that Alistair Moffat, the son of Jack and Ellen Moffat?' The voice was oddly formal and certainly not familiar. 'I'm calling from Kelso, from your parents' house. There's no easy way to say this but –'

I cut him off: 'Is it my Ma or my Dad?'

'It's your father, I'm afraid, early this evening.'

I cut him off again. 'Tell my Ma I'll be there, tonight.' It was 6 February 1986.

The blizzard had begun to blow itself out by the time I reached Fairshiels, but the snow was so thick and drifted that it was difficult to know where the road was. I stopped the car at a phone box, found the tarmac with a shovel I'd shoved in the back, and then called the police at Lauder to tell them I was coming over Soutra and ask if their patrol cars could look out for me. Crunching through the virgin snow, it was surprisingly easy to climb up to the plateau, and when the road levelled off, the moon broke a smoky hole through the clouds. It flooded the landscape with a chilling monochrome light, bouncing off the white ground. My children always teased me on Soutra when I took them to Kelso to see their Grandpa Jack and Grannie Ellen. 'This is the bit where Dad's accent changes.' And in the back seat they would begin chanting, 'Aye, grand day,' 'What fettle?' and other phrases that used to baffle them. I realised I had raised city kids whose laughter could call up for me the first weeks away at university where I mangled my Border vowels and tumbled into a dozen mouthtraps like 'a can of lager' or a stream of expletives on the rugby pitch uttered in search of the 'ba''. But my children were right. Somewhere after leaving Midlothian and before descending into Lauderdale I used to experience a no-syncromesh linguistic gear-change when my expression crashed through from an acquired version of Scots middle class to the Border dialect I grew up with, a language that described my childhood, and the place I always went back to, the place I never ceased to call home, or hame.

More than ten years before I drove through the blizzard, the phone had rung very late in my grubby flat in London, where I had been doing a postgraduate degree at the university, still learning to speak English, still in the process of leaving my child-hood behind. 'Come home, son.' It was my Ma. 'I need you to come home right away, son. Your Dad's been taken ill. He's at the Western General now. They're operating.' I had left imme-diately to catch the night train from King's Cross. It had been the first of the long journeys back.

At the top of the stairs at 42 Inchmead Drive, my Dad had suffered a sudden, violent headache and crashed all his length, falling right to the bottom. A massive stroke had flooded his brain with blood. After a long time in hospital in Edinburgh he had come home badly paralysed and half blind. Despite Herculean efforts, he never regained anything remotely close to his old vigour and stature. In fact it is now an effort to remem-ber what he was like in the time before he became ill. The stroke had somehow allowed his emotions to surface more easily and the stern, even violent man who raised me often burst into tears, sometimes provoked by nothing more than a smile. While he had lost none of his intellectual abilities, his feelings clouded his thinking so much that his old directness was muted and his curiosity satisfied by staring for hours at the television. Once when I sat close by him on the sofa and clumsily tried to console him, he used his good arm to push me away: 'Get away. Get away from me. Bugger off.'

I hated to see him so brutally diminished, and felt sincere pity for him, something he himself would have hated. It was a start-ling reversal – from a straight-backed, good-looking man to a shrivelled invalid. My Dad's dominant ill nature, impatience and vehemently held opinions were all blunted, bottled up inside a hunched figure, propped by a stick and often showing the defeated, vacant expression of the permanently disabled.

Our dealings with each other had been changing anyway. Even into my middle teenage years my Dad had never hesitated to hit me, sometimes winding me, drawing blood from a lip more than once. But as I grew taller, thickened out and became able to do more than merely defend myself, some instinct in him had persuaded my Dad to back off. Perhaps the risk of a very violent and sustained exchange was too great, something that would have exploded our family. And something that my Ma and my Gran would not have tolerated. Or perhaps it went deeper. The possibility of defeat, of humiliation at the hands of his son may have appeared all too real. Everyone on our council estate knew of fathers who had made the mistake of pushing their growing sons once too often and suffered unexpected consequences. In front of their families, within the crowded space of their small houses, they had been transformed from the strongest to the weakest in the time it takes to throw a punch. And the balance of a family had been irrevocably tipped against nature.

But without a blow being struck, as a consequence of a leaky blood vessel, everything between my Dad and me had changed, and when I looked at his scarred head, his drooping, dribbling face, his crooked, pathetic smile, it felt as though he had died once already.

As often, on the southern slopes of Soutra Hill the narrow cleft of the young Leader Water had caught less snow and I began to make better time. Carfraemill, Thirlestane, Gordon, Nenthorn and then the pale glow of the lights of Kelso, hunkered down out of sight amongst the folded ridges above the Tweed.

As I drove up the empty street in the moonlit snow, the house at No. 42 looked cold, ghostly and forbidding. Her neighbour, Margaret Boyd, was sitting with my Ma, who perched on the edge of the armchair by the fireplace, hunched over, smoking and staring at the floor. In that moment I could see a long landscape of love disappearing behind her, and a tunnel of bleakness in front. My parents had argued all through our childhood, often about nothing more than disappointment, but she seemed diminished now, wrapped in her own arms, suddenly crined in on herself, small and all alone.

Margaret Boyd offered to call my wife and ask her to let the Lauder police know I'd made it through the blizzard. Very slowly my Ma uncurled, and very gently she let me hold her and kiss her. But she never cried, not one tear was shed. Instead it all stayed dammed behind granite impassivity, a private grief so immense that no word or sign could articulate it. Much later I ceased to wonder at that, because I understood, despite everything, how much she loved him, no matter what he said, did or was.

'Where is my Dad, Ma?' Margaret's husband, Adam, was a forester with a native strength that had enabled him to carry my Dad upstairs and lay him out on his bed. The room had no fire. His cheeks were cold and when I took his hand his huge fingers fell through my grip. Absurdly I had a powerful sense that this wouldn't have happened if I'd been here. He was only seventy. I could even have fixed it, caught him before he fell, held him fast, steadied him, not let his heart burst. For reasons I can't even intuit now I lay down next to him on the bed, to hold him close as he had never let me hold him while he lived, somehow to find a way to finish it with him.

After a time beyond remembering someone tapped quietly on the bedroom door. It was Margaret: 'Alistair, you've left your car running.' I got into the driver's seat to cut the engine, and staring out along the familiar, empty and echoic street, I realised that in my mind I had made this journey many times, and that some day my son would make the same journey.

After my Dad's funeral I spent time with my Ma. It seemed like a good thing to talk over the past and I began to repeat some of the stories my Grannie had told me about her early life. 'Your Dad never told me very much at all,' she said, 'but what your Grannie told you son, it's mostly lies. She made up things. I don't know where she came from but her stories never really tallied. She told you a lot of nonsense.'

I felt hollow. All those nights long ago as she lay next to me, her head close behind mine on the bolster pillow, whispering, she invented a world for me. Instead of giving me a real past, a proper genealogy of the sort she constructed for everyone else, she made one up, covered over a secret she kept from me all of my life. At the time I was angry, I thought she had cheated me. But now, as I write this, knowing what I know and understanding something of her world and her long life, I love her again for her kindness in denying herself the luxury of uttering the bitter truths she lived with.

'And I suppose you know,' said my Ma, lighting another cigarette, 'that your Dad had no Dad of his own. He was illegitimate.'

I didn't, or at least I hadn't put it all together. But it fitted. Throughout my childhood I wanted to be like everybody else, just like the Taylors, the Halls, the Witherses, even the Woodheads, and like the freckled boy in the grey school cap who smiled up at his pipe-smoking, smiling Dad as they stepped out together on a father-and-son jaunt somewhere exciting, but safe. Somewhere my Dad and I never went. And when they came back home, his Mum had made their cheery tea, with Oxo cubes, and everything seemed to go swimmingly, a seamless summer of happy days and smily faces, where everything fell exactly into place. Exactly. Normal. Cosy. No Bad Things. Not like my family, at least my Dad and me. In a sustained childish quest for normality, comfortable, reassuring continuity, I became obsessed by names, sensed somehow that they were the key to happiness. Names linked relatives together, even if they weren't the same names. From an early age I understood the concept of maiden names, that women were obliged to change their names the minute they got married and started with the Oxo cubes. When my Grannie answered my persistent enquiries about the whereabouts of her maiden name by telling me that it was Jeffrey, I found it unconvincing, empty of the reassurance I so desperately sought, thought it a strange coincidence that it was also the surname of the two spinster sisters who had moved in next door after Auntie Grey and Uncle Bob had gone. And when she used stories to avoid all the callow questions I continually put to her, I only sensed that she had a buried secret that had to be kept hidden. But something had held me back from articulating it, from asking a direct question.

Now I know my Dad was a bastard, a blunt fact buried inside him that framed his life, formed his attitudes and ensured that he never found any settled contentment. Having had no father of his own, he had no first-hand idea of how to deal with my adolescent refusals, my backchat or his own anger at my shortcomings. Stung by my insolence he lashed out often and sometimes painfully. Once he hit me during an argument in the living room and I finished on the kitchenette floor, scattering the chairs.

After a bad row had subsided, a terrible silence sometimes descended. Simmering looks were exchanged and my Ma would sit by the fire, hugging herself, rocking, shaking her head at the pain and the elemental anger that exploded so often and so readily. At these times she said the only thing she could say, that if we did not stop fighting, arguing and constantly looking for fault, then she would pack her bags and leave us. This panicked Barbara, Marjie and me, and we begged her not to abandon us, implored her to stay, promised to behave better, not to rouse Dad into rages, swallow our refusals, try to be like other families who never carried on like this, but lived douce, comforting, calm and uneventful lives.

One of eight children brought up in a tiny tenement flat in crowded, cosmopolitan Hawick, my Ma understood and intuited much more about the give and take of family life than my Dad who, it turned out, was an only child raised in a household of women whose experience was first framed in farm places and the fields around. Ma was busy, bustling, coping, got on with life, and she loved us first and asked questions later.

My Dad asked questions first and if we supplied the right answers then he might love us, but there was no way we would know since he lacked the emotional vocabulary to say it. All my life he only ever touched me in anger. Yet despite that, I realised that I desperately wanted him to love me, to protect me. As a dreamy toddler my sister Barbara once wandered into the main road in front of an oncoming lorry and in an instant he dived all his length, snatched her from under the roaring wheels and rolled to the other side of the road. I knew he could do that, without thinking. But I also knew that he could just as easily betray me, run me down in front of other people, seem to despise me for my weakness, not love me at all.

Of course there were reasons, if not excuses. Much of my Dad's angry competitiveness was born out of his own disappointments. At Kelso High School in 1930 he came first in the A class at Mathematics and English, beating a future principal of a Scottish university. But circumstances forced him to leave school as soon as he legally could. At fourteen he needed to find work to support his Mother. My Dad became an electrician, while others with less ability but one more parent went to the university in Edinburgh, got jobs in the bank, did better. If the memory of our rows and his rages ring louder in my head than anything else, I now know it is because they are an echo of his own upbringing. 'Bastard. Bastard. Bastard' and other names were called after him in the school playground and up the road home. Even into adulthood my Dad had a reputation for being emphatic with his fists. He had to be, to survive and keep alive some self respect for himself and for Bina. The corner boys would have spat insults about his Mother and when he waded into them, he would have hurt one or two before they got him to the ground. The bond between Bina and her only child must have been immense, unspoken and impossible for me to understand as I grew up. But sometimes his competitiveness surfaced in eccentric ways and he did astonishing things which no-one could have predicted.

In 1955 my Dad drove down our street in a car. It was a black post-war Model T-type Ford and he carefully parked it outside

outside a cottage with steep pitched red wooden eaves. It stood by itself deep in the pine woods that surrounded the policies. I remember an old man in a waistcoat with a gold watch chain who wore his bunnet in the house. The brown paper blinds in the front room were drawn against the afternoon sun. He and his wife had just cleared away Sunday lunch and she made me a plate of mashed potatoes and gravy. As I ate, with a spoon, in the kitchen, the old man and my Dad talked in low voices in the front room while the woman sat opposite me and beamed as I shovelled down the mash and thick brown gravy. She kept telling me how like my Dad I was. I didn't say anything. Then the old man came through and asked Bella where their tea was. Bella. That's all I can remember. My Dad took me more than once but never told me who these people were. Bella just kept looking and smiling at me and giving me things to eat.

The five-and-a-half-day week was still standard for tradesmen in the Fifties and early Sixties and my Dad always worked on Saturday mornings. He often took me with him in the van and if we were ever anywhere nearby we went to the Kames, a big house in Berwickshire. Daisy Lauder, a kindly middle-aged lady, was the Housekeeper and her father John, the Head Gardener. I knew that because I asked them. Dad never explained anything – even when I asked him why his middle name was the same as their surname, he told me to shut up. Bina told me that she had given him the name because she liked the town, but I was sure that she had never been there. My Dad was fond of Daisy and John and often brought things thrown out by the toffs which he had reconditioned: an electric kettle and a hoover and once, to Daisy's open-mouthed amazement, an electric blanket. We took away boxes of vegetables and John always cut some flowers in season for us to take to Bina. On a blazing hot Saturday I remember he took me to the greenhouses inside the walled garden. Even with all the vents open and the roof blinds rolled down, it was stifling. He grew grapes – the vines climbed the walls and arched over the roof to make it shady – as well as peaches, apricots and greengages. The scent of them has never left me. One autumn Saturday morning Daisy gave me a big biscuit tin full of mushrooms which my Gran cooked when we got back to Kelso. Bina loved mushrooms and I vividly remember the taste and the black juice in the pan. Another time we brought back a brace of rabbits which she took out the back and laid on the lid of the coal bunker. With an axe the rabbits were decapitated, the paws nipped off, and after slitting the skin up the belly, my Gran gripped each carcase and tore back the skin. I was rapt, open-mouthed. Pulling out the liver and lights, she laid them in a soup plate and then cut up the skinned rabbits for the stewpot.

During this flurry of expert butchery Bina was full of questions for my Dad about Daisy and her family. These were questions no-one else was allowed to understand. At least not until now, more than forty years later, not until I gave myself the time to think about the mysteries swirling around Bina and her son.

TEN

Reliable Memories

'MY, IS HE not like his Father.' 'Yes, and all that white hair, just like when his Dad was small. The very picture.' 1950s women seemed huge to me, wore rustling, swishy skirts, high heels, nylons, hats, and had shiny black handbags bursting with compacts, long-handled combs, cigarettes and very small hankies. When out visiting, particularly at New Year, they also applied a great deal of make-up, red lipstick and even more perfume. Around them and their gush of commonplaces hung a dizzying, headachey atmosphere. If you ventured too near, compulsory kisses were planted in forced clinches, pungent, wet and repulsive. The more you wriggled the more they clasped you closer to the source of the awful, womany smell, and when they took a good hold, their soft, curvy, pastel shapes turned out to be invisibly in elastic armour.

'Same bad temper as well,' when I prised off the red-painted claws and made a break through the cigarette clouds for the living room door. None of the perfumed, upholstered women ever said I was like my Ma, or even like Bina. As the teacups rattled in the saucers and the ashtray smouldered, it was always the same: 'Two peas in a pod.'

But what pod? My sister, Barbara stopped wondering about all of these secrets, and two years ago began a more practical approach by acquiring copies of Bina's and her son's birth certificates and one or two other pieces of documentary evidence. They prompted a long, laborious search through thickets of unindexed records: the early censuses, registers of births, marriages and deaths, parish and school attendance records, the great Statistical Accounts of Scotland and much else. But even when some of the entries made sense and appeared to lead somewhere, they were like pieces of an unmade jigsaw, mostly incomprehensible without the picture on the box to guide us. Such documentary evidence as Barbara and I could find supplied only the bare bones of dates and places of birth, and where doubts and ignorance existed, there were only blank spaces, no stories or explanations, no sense that the copperplate entries described the span of real experience, traced the warmth of real people. I needed more background, more first-hand understanding of Bina's and Dad's lives before I could use birth and death certificates properly, or make sense of census returns or parish registers. And for that I went to talk to one of the few people still alive who could remember more than facts and who would not simply recite unreliable memories.

Jean Gladstone used to visit us at No. 42 every Tuesday night without fail. To the regular annoyance of my sisters and me, the telly was switched off, tea brewed and conversation made. Jean, Bina and my Ma exchanged the week's news, and smoked cigarettes while we lay on the floor doing extra homework. In her Seventies now, Jean lives by herself in the same house on the same council estate at the foot of the Meadows, not far from where the Double Bump used to be. I phoned to fix a time to come and see her.

Driving down to Kelso to see Jean, I went over and over the void at the heart of my family. If I looked like my Dad (and I do), then whom did he take after (certainly not Bina)? Gran was dark, big-made and soft-featured while Dad was slim and very fair with an angular, distinctive face. Where did that handsome face come from? Who gave it to him? If he had lived longer, my Father would have been thunderstruck to know how his grandson, my son Adam, grew into a man. In my mind I can see the three of us together in an impossible photograph, three men unmistakably grandfather, son and grandson. But there was always a fourth figure missing, someone whose absence dominated the impossible photograph. The ghost of my grandfather.

'Oh yes,' said Jean, 'your Dad looked very like him. So do you.' She smiled at my waiting silence and shook her head. 'Well, I suppose it doesn't matter now.' Wrong, Jean, it matters very much. 'It was Bob Charters, Robert Charters. He got your Grannie pregnant. When he was on leave from the war.' Mental arithmetic whirred. 1916. 30 January 1916 was the date of my Dad's birth. That means Bina and Robert Charters were lovers in May 1915. So he was a soldier, briefly home from the unimaginable, murderous madness of the trenches. When was the Somme? Ypres? 1916? Where was he in 1915? What did he do? How did he survive? Did he? What happened to him?

Jean and I did more arithmethic. Bina was twenty-four, a time-served seamstress at Lugton and Porteous of Kelso, tailor to the landed and middle classes. I have two photographs of her from around that time, found amongst many of Ma and Dad in an old cigar box. For some forgotten dance or party she is wearing a fancy-dress costume, something almost certainly run up at home out of remnants. 'She always had clever hands, your Grannie.' A long, full-length skirt is drawn in at her narrow waist by a lacy cummerbund and the bodice is cut bolero-style to show off an embroidered panelled blouse with puffed sleeves gathered at the wrist. Pinned to Bina's hair is a large, starched linen head-dress, like an elevated version of an old-fashioned nurse's cap.

The photographs are two different shots taken at the same session. The more yellowed and fading shows Bina standing with her left hand on her hip, no doubt parked there by the photographer for a standard pose, and her weight on the right leg. Tall and straight, Bina stares directly at the lens without inhibition, her face in easy repose. Long dark hair is centre-parted and plaited and ribboned to her waist. Across ninety years, the span of three generations, I can see her clearly in her fancy dress, the old woman who raised me. She is looking out at me from our past, near the beginning of her own life. A soft, soft face, an artless girl from country places who stands perfectly still for the fussing photographer. In the second picture, Bina sits and looks camera-left. The resolution is much clearer and her unlined features look dream-like, distant, far away somewhere in her future. Perhaps she hears herself whispering to me on the bolster pillow, telling me stories of parties and dances and fancy dress, remembering the giggling excitements of nights out and the ghosts of long-gone summers. I can feel her with me now, stroking my hair, wrapping me in her warmth. I know the girl in the photographs, when I was a little boy I was friends with her, because the old woman told me almost everything about her. Almost everthing, except the most important thing. The incident that defined her whole adult life, what made the soft-faced lass weep many tears.

When Robert Charters came home from Hell in May 1915, he made love to my Gran somewhere in the spring countryside around Kelso. Circumstances almost invariably forced young lovers outdoors in those days and records remember a warm and unusually sunny start to the summer of 1915. Quiet secluded walks in the light evenings were common enough to name those secret places, and before it become the prosaic Inch Road, a path through the fields to the north of the town was known as Love Lane. Perhaps Robert walked there with his soft-faced lass in the evening sunshine. Perhaps the waiting, looming carnage in Flanders persuaded him of last chances, lost lives, wasted promises and recklessness. It is not difficult to imagine their conversation. Perhaps Bina loved him anyway, whatever he said. I hope so.

When Robert caught the train to take him back to his unit, back to the crazy summer of the trenches, he must have looked at the Tweed Valley trundling past the carriage window, wondering if he would ever see its sunlit peace again. Already many had died, and many more would take the ghost road home.

Jean Gladstone told me a chilling story about my grandfather. In the winter of 1915–16 Robert Charters was working in a tunnel when the Germans filled it with mustard gas. Men close by began to scream seconds before it affected him. Somehow he crawled out, gasping, rasping for air before the medical orderlies got to him. He was quickly moved behind the lines. His blisters healed, but despite a long period in an army hospital he never recovered his health, and spent the rest of his life as a semi-invalid.

During his convalescence word reached Robert from Kelso that Bina was pregnant. This news made life very complicated. After his brief affair with my Gran, it appears that Robert had gone on to form a relationship with another young woman, Christina Sanderson, the woman he would ultimately marry. In May 1915 reckless promiscuity and bad luck had presented him with a life-changing decision, a choice which would affect four lives, those of three adults and one unborn baby. In the event brutal practicalities determined the outcome. It turned out that Bina had not the means to compel Robert to choose her, even though she was pregnant by him, for I discovered that she herself had been an illegitimate child and could call on no father for support or to demand settlement of some sort. From a lengthy and painstaking search through unindexed census returns for the second half of the nineteenth century, I had also discovered the buried identity of my great-grandmother, Annie Moffat, Bina's mother. Until I found her in the copperplate list of entries, I did not even know her name. Succeeding censuses show that Annie had worked all her long life at farm places, and when she fell pregnant in March 1890, her family closed around and Bina was, like me, raised by her grandmother while her mother went out to work. It was the first inkling I had of repeating patterns from a hidden past.

Unlike Bina, Christina Sanderson came from a well-set Kelso family who ran a prosperous bakery business in Simon Square. Sandy Sanderson was a forthright character and he would have wasted little time with niceties. Whatever else had happened in the past was past and Robert Charters was engaged to his daughter, and that was that. They were married in March 1916. A few weeks earlier, on 30 January, my Dad had been born. The birth certificate noted 'Father Unknown'. Except he wasn't. Across the town his father and the new Mrs Charters set up home and set out on their life together.

The bitter intensity of what my Gran felt in those hard early years can only be guessed at. Robert Charters' choice, his marriage and new family were not remote events happening outside the circle of her own life, but something close at hand and in plain sight – for everyone to comment on. Bina must have felt hollow, a woman used and rejected. Lacked the gumption and the means to compel her child's father to marry her. And everyone who lived in Kelso knew that she had been used and rejected. That is a polite version of the sort of language they would have uttered, perhaps even openly and in my Gran's hearing. When Annie gave birth to Bina in 1890 the Moffats lived on a farm, at Cliftonhill near Kelso, and the circumstances were very different. In small country communities illegitimacy was not considered such a grievous stain, and indeed a new pair of growing hands was often welcome. But more than that, there were many fewer people at Cliftonhill to know and disapprove, if they did, and in any case Annie and her family regularly moved away and on to a different job on another farm. Judgement tended not to trail around behind them. In towns it was not like that. In 1916 Kelso was small enough for everyone to know everyone else's business and large enough to impose a continuing sense of shame and ridicule which could press hard on a person who, like my Grannie, had so obviously failed. And then there was the Kirk, the Church of Scotland, to institutionalise that disapproval. Partly in order to ease the months old. She is Nan Lauder, named after my great-grand-mother, Annie, and her surname became my Dad's middle name. Glowering, gripping the backrail, stands Daisy Lauder, her elder sister, the generous woman who gave me a biscuit tin box of mushrooms for Bina. These simple facts are discoveries, not observations, astonishing discoveries revealed only when I began to ask questions of Jean Gladstone. When I saw the pictures as a child, my Gran would only say that these children belonged to friends. She couldn't remember who they were, she said, looking away out of the window, not any of them. They turned out to be very much more than friends, as I found out later.

The second photograph is a single portrait of my Dad sitting on a stone pedestal, perhaps two years old, chubby and quizzical. A year later he has grown noticeably taller and stands next to Annie, his Gran, the old woman who brought him up, and he has in his fist a small Union Jack on a stick. Daisy Lauder is on Annie's right and the old lady holds fidgeting little Nan still, wedged between her knees. Unusually the shot was taken outside and by the length of the grass and the look of the trees, it seems to have been late summer. The year was 1919. Annie Moffat was sixty-one years old and wisps of her greying hair blow free in the breeze. Her expression is steady, unwavering. Jaw set, mouth clamped shut, she stares passive-aggressively at the lens. Perhaps like most people she hated having her picture taken. Written on her dour, granite face are the years of the hard, day-in, day-out toil of the farm labourer, the bondager that she was. But despite the grim aspect, what is striking about the photograph is the hands. My Dad cuddles into his Gran, his right hand high on her shoulder. Annie holds Nan gently with her thick, arthritic fingers while Daisy leans into her with casual affection. This is a portrait of part of a close family, something obvious to anyone who sees it. Except me. When I asked who those people were with my Dad (for it was undeniably him), I was told repeatedly that they were not important, only friends. My great-grandmother stared out, looking straight at me, but she was condemned to be forgotten as an anonymous friend, someone without identity. As late as the 1950s the ripples of Robert and Bina's moment of passion washed over the life of a curious little boy, relegating his past to something better ignored than explained.

At the foot of Union Street, near my Dad's birthplace at No. 9, stood the steamie, Kelso's communal laundry. After baby John was weaned, Bina found a job there doing other people's washing. Out of that she built up a sideline repairing and sometimes making clothes for other people, and on Mondays she walked up to the Poorhouse to do darning and mending. When Jean Gladstone told me that, in 1919, after the Armistice, Bina was employed as a maid at Floors Castle, I remembered some of her tales, what she whispered to me as I cuddled in close. Walking two miles through the early dark of the winter, she was one of the first at work and her job included lighting the morning fires. And that detail lit a smile inside me. I remembered her stories about working alone in the castle, the tale of the ghostly old lady, and the linen napkins. My Ma was wrong. Bina hadn't made it all up, she just missed out bits, never explained the circumstances.

ELEVEN

Family

'YOU'D BETTER GO round and speak to Meg Robertson.' On the morning after my Dad's death in February 1986, my Ma looked up at me and out of whatever distant redoubt she had found so that she could give me an errand. 'She'll want to see you, not want to be told by somebody else.' News of a death always ricocheted round a small town like Kelso without the need for the bereaved to inform anyone. People came to No. 42 to see my Ma, my sisters and me without being asked, unafraid of what they might find, not tentative or awkward over muttered condolences, but supportive and sensible. A neighbour brought some soup, someone else did some shopping. But Meg Robertson had to be told, and by me and no-one else.

When I was a little boy I called her Auntie Meg and spent time playing in her house round at Inch Road. It was one of the few places not needing Bina's permission. But I never thought anything of what I called Meg. Auntie Grey and Uncle Bob lived next door at No. 44 and they were no relation. For many years I assumed that Auntie Meg Robertson was only a term of familiarity. However, as often with my family, the truth turned up eventually, and in heavy disguise.

Meg had of course heard the news before I arrived, and she was weeping when her husband Jim brought me into the living room. Immediately I saw that this was no corner-of-the-hankie business. Meg was hurting at my Dad's death, sitting in her chair, crying in gasping sobs. And even though our culture discourages such things, I went to hold her in an awkward embrace as she sat with her hands in her lap. 'You're so like him, so like your Dad, so like him,' Meg whispered to me over and over, 'just the same voice, just the same, just like him.' Jim Robertson stood beside us with his hand clapping his wife's shoulder, smiling a tight-lipped smile of grim comfort, waiting for the pain to subside.

Meg did not come to the funeral and I never saw her again before she herself died. Some unexplained feud had exploded between my Dad and Jim Robertson which forced his wife's sadness to remain private. All that my Ma could tell me was that Dad was somehow raised alongside her, perhaps as neighbours, but she had no idea if they were related or not. Two years ago Jean Gladstone told me the truth, the real reason why Meg had wept so bitterly at the news of my Dad's death. She had lost her brother.

At almost exactly the same time as Bina had given birth to my Dad another illegitimate baby was brought into the world in Kelso. But she was not so fortunate. Either as a result of her mother's death or her inability or unwillingness to cope with the child, Margaret or Meg Weatherstone became destitute, and as a consequence, the responsibility of the parish poor relief fund. When a foster-home was sought for Meg, Violet Middlemas, the lady in charge of the disbursement of the fund, approached Bina. And of course she was sympathetic. But in the tenement flat they had moved to at 10 Horsemarket from Union Street, it was Annie who took responsibility and began to raise her alongside my Dad.

As ever with the Moffats it was an intimate nurture. I did not know it when Meg sobbed against my shoulder, but both of us had slept with Bina, had been wrapped in her warmth and listened to her stories. And at the same time, in their big double bed, my Dad cuddled up to his mother. Meg and my Dad were part of the same household until the late 1930s when marriage and war took them both away. All of their formative experiences happened side by side; they learned to walk across the same floor, to form first words, they went to school with each other, found work, boyfriends, girlfriends at the same time, were siblings in everything but blood. And I and my sisters knew nothing whatever of this, and another piece of our family was literally denied to us.

There exists a photograph of the brother and his adopted sister. It was found in an envelope amongst Bina's things after her death and was taken in the yard behind the tenement at Horsemarket. The likely date is the summer of 1927 or 1928, and between them Meg and my Dad hold a very young Jenny Lauder, the little sister of Nan and Daisy. All three of them are squinting against an evening sun. Unlike the earlier shots of my Dad and Bina, this is not a professional studio portrait but something snapped by a neighbour with a Box Brownie, or one of the other cameras beginning to become available to ordinary people. Across more than seventy years, it transmits a documentary reality missing in the earlier photographs. The children appear to be shy but happy, and their smiles are natural, not the cheesy grimaces or the deadpan of the posed studio shots. And once again hands are eloquent, especially Meg's as she uses both to steady Jenny. My Dad wears a shirt and jumper, his face well scrubbed for the occasion, and Meg has on a dark velvet dress with embroidery at the square-cut neck. This last was likely made on my Gran's Singer sewing machine and she often ran up summer dresses for Nan, Meg and Jenny. Using remnants and her big pinking shears, she could cut, pin, fit and sew together one of these in a matter of hours – much to the delight of the wee girls. Once she made a boy's suit for my Dad, which he promptly ruined by rolling about on the floor of the cinema known as the Tin Kirk. Turnout for the children in her care was important for Bina and she used her clever hands to make them look as well put on as any, whoever their parents might be.

★

My researches did add some substance to the cold statistics of the census, and birth and death certificates. With Jean Gladstone's help I found out that Nan Lauder was still living, in fact hale and happy in a small council house in Tweedmouth, near Berwick. Even though I had never before spoken to Nan, she opened the door to her flat and greeted me like family, as someone already familiar with all the names and relationships, someone she had been thinking about throughout her immense life. When I first met Nan in 1999, we kissed, and normally full of chatter and smoothing pleasantries, I found I couldn't speak for a moment. Both of us made our way awkwardly into her sitting room without a word and sat down. And when I looked up, I could see that the old lady had tears in her eyes. I smiled through mine and it felt as though a wide circle had completed itself, against all odds. Perhaps the old ties of love and blood were not yet gone. She explained that she and her sisters Daisy and Jenny were second cousins to Bina. But in an everyday reality they were much closer to each other than that. The little girls had spent their childhood summers living in Kelso with Bina, my Dad and Meg, and Nan added that her mother, Maggie-Anne Lauder, had a particularly strong bond with Bina's mother Annie Moffat. In fact they were more like mother and child than aunt and niece because my great-grandmother had raised Maggie-Anne whose natural mother, Bella, had gone away to become a housekeeper at a big farm. Nan also had a great deal to say about the old life on the land, and her stories imparted some humanity to the scatter of dates and places. In particular she could remember what her mother told her about Cliftonhill Farm, near Kelso, and what life there in the 1890s was like.

The Moffats' cottage, as Nan described it, stood south-facing at the top of a gentle slope down to the meandering Eden Water. Later I visited the place myself: at the farm cows still graze the water meadow by the little river as it loops around the foot of

Ednam Hill before tumbling absent-mindedly into the Tweed below Kelso. Bina's first summer blazed with light and heat. Records show an early harvest that year and more than one cut of sweet-smelling hay. Even though she was much too young to remember it, the warmth of 1891 at Cliftonhill was printed on Bina Moffat's soul.

She loved what she called 'farm places', and decades later when my Dad took her for a run in the car around country roads she had nothing much to say, only staring out of the passenger window across the evening fields and on beyond them to the darker heads of the Cheviots. 'Aye,' she murmured quietly when it was time for my Dad to move on. If I had been more attentive and less impatient, sliding about on the back seat, I might have noticed my Gran remembering the old life.

It is all gone now, barely catchable in the fading memories of those who watched the big horses in their high-peaked collars leading in the harvest, or saw a dozen women singling turnips in the same field, their voices carrying clear across the Eden in the still of the evening. But Bina knew it. She watched the old life pass her cottage door. When she was only four or five and could swing a stout stick and roar loud enough, she became an active part of it, herding ewes or prodding the cows in for evening milking. Even into old age she never lost the rhythms of the countryside, always up early in the spring and summer time, sleeping later in the winter. Or its language; at the start of the working day she often looked at me and said, 'well, let's get yokit,' and its end was always 'lowsin' time', terms taken straight from the old culture of horseworking. And to my childish amazement she could tell approximately what time of day it was without looking at the clock and she never wore a wristwatch. The day was what interested Bina, not the hour.

My older daughter is like her great grandmother. Helen loves the Borders landscape, has the patience and presence of a maturity far in front of her years, and is at home with the big horses and the country places she takes them to. And every now and then, on the edge of her smile, I see Bina again.

The 1891 Census return for Cliftonhill is valedictory, a snapshot taken in the evening years of high farming in Scotland. In 9 family houses the enumerator counted 62 people living on the farm; 23 of them worked there full time and raised 25 children, many of whom would have done regular herding jobs and helped at hay-making and harvest. With the advances in mechanisation, the effect of the First World War on manpower, and the growing unpopularity of farm work in general, the agricultural population declined sharply after 1891. Now Cliftonhill Farm is run by only two people, Archie and Maggie Stewart. What was once the consoling work of many hands can now be an entirely solitary activity. The steading has modern machinery and new buildings, but behind the steel, the breeze blocks and the corrugated roofs lie the remains of the past. The agricultural archaeology of Cliftonhill is very poignant: old and ruined cottages, a long and well-built stable for at least ten heavy horses, rows of arched cartsheds mostly blocked up, a huge hay barn and perhaps most atmospheric of all, old fireplaces in buildings recently converted to other uses. Only silence now where 25 children shrieked and careered, where four pairs of Clydesdales clattered out to the fields and where more than 20 people had a quiet smoke and a blether at lowsin' time.

But Annie and her sister Mary Moffat worked hard, and on days of rain and worse on Ednam Hill their lives would have seemed less than Edenic. The nine bondagers at Cliftonhill did most of the muddy, unattractive tasks left to them by the men. What the romantic poets, painters like Constable and particularly Robert Burns forgot is how utterly farming depended on the labour of women, and how profoundly it changed when they began to leave the land. But compared to the neurotic, centrally-heated existence we have now, it was a wholesome sort of life; they ate when they were hungry, slept when they were tired and died when they were worn out.

Throughout the summer of 1999 that I spent searching for my shadow family, I found little that was substantial, little that marked their presence in the past. It was as though the fields and pastures of the Tweed Valley were like the sea, unchanging, cold and pitiless. And the lives of Annie, her sisters, brother and parents had been submerged, their spirits entirely fled. Nan Lauder listened to me talk about how the shadows of our family seemed to flit across the landscape and how difficult it was to catch much sense of the pungency of their lives. And then she quietly told me where to look, somewhere so obvious that I had missed it completely. Assuming that farm workers would never have been able to afford such a thing, I had not checked the lists of headstones in the churchyards around Kelso. After all, my Dad had not been able to pay for one for Bina.

Nan rewound the story back to Bina's birth in December 1890. After Christmas with her new baby girl, work took Annie out of the family cottage and into the winter fields, and Bina herself went into the care of Maggie, her grandmother. But their time together was cut cruelly short. At sixty-four the old woman was failing and on 17 February 1891 Margaret Moffat died. My great-great-grandfather William determined on a proper memorial for his beloved wife and unusually for a ploughman he managed to scrape sufficient cash together for a lair in Ednam kirkyard and an imposing tombstone. The kirk stands at the heart of the village at the western foot of Cliftonhill, and it is very old, worship having taken place there for at least a thousand years. I found the headstone easily enough at the end of a row in a corner of the graveyard, not far from the old church. When he counted out the money to commission the memorial, William made sure that the sculptor left enough room for his name and those of his family. And there they were, chiselled in flaky sandstone, the names of my people, the span of their lives, my blood family. 'Erected by WILLIAM MOFFAT in memory of his wife, MARGARET JAFFREY, who died at Clifton Hill 17.2.1891 aged 64 years also the above WILLIAM MOFFAT who died at

Wormerlaw 1.3.1896 aged 69 years also his daughter MARY who died at Kelso 20.1.1920 aged 56 years also their eldest daughter ISABELLA who died at Kelso 11.1.1931 aged 78 years.' When she was young Bina knew them all, and my Dad knew his aunts, Mary and Isabella, they lived in the same house in Horsemarket with him. But all I had was an ancient silence, a cold stone in a damp kirkyard and a chiselled inscription. Just names, no inherited memories, nothing passed on. In all the long time I spent looking for my family, chasing shadows, scouring records, the moment when I read and re-read William Moffat's headstone in Ednam churchyard was the moment I felt most cheated, most angry, most disappointed. I couldn't have known my great-great-grandfather or my great-aunts, they all died long before I was born, but I could have known *about* them, through Bina and my Dad. I could have had some second-hand but close sense of their lives, what they were like, some stories, bits of daftness, the things they said and did. But it was all too late, much too late. I tried hard to find something for myself in the inscription, something I was able to take away with me, and all that came was cold formality. Bones not flesh. But when I turned to walk back to my car, I stopped for a moment and immediately saw what Bina and my Dad saw when they came with the hearse to Ednam kirkyard in 1920 and 1931 to bury Mary and Isabella. The gravestone faces east, towards the morning sun, the rigs at up Cliftonhill Farm and stretching towards the distant sea, the rich, red earth of Berwickshire where many generations of my family had walked their lives. And for a fleeting instant I heard them, my old aunts, heard the clatter of their boots come down the hill, on the metalled road by the old smiddy, heard their quiet morning chatter as they shouldered their hoes and pushed open the gate to the turnips in the bottom field by the River Eden.

Epilogue: Days of Memory

AFTER MY MA died in 1990, I no longer had any family reason to come back down to the Borders. Hers was the last departure. My sisters had gone long before, to live in England, and while it was good to see my Hawick cousins, the middle years gap between weddings and funerals meant that there were few formal occasions when we came together. And, of course, I had no relatives in Kelso, at least none to speak of. I missed that journey to the Borders very much, found it difficult to call Edinburgh home, beautiful city though it is.

In my work as a television executive I travelled a great deal: up and down from Edinburgh to London on the shuttle, to France twice a year and the USA more often. And I disliked it all very much. Perhaps the most unpleasant destination was Cannes on the French Riviera. In April and October two huge television markets are held in a concrete bunker by the seaside known as Le Palais des Festivals. It is a profoundly ugly, brutal building. There are no windows and as the weary, overfed and irritable delegates come up to street level, they blink into the Mediterranean sunshine. Despite the weather and the setting, Cannes is ugly. The front consists in a row of designer shops entirely without character and a group of so-called great hotels, and behind them are anonymous blocks and rectilinear streets leading to a motorway. The hotels advertise luxury and sophistication but are in fact efficient machines for processing people and large quantities of their money. Not one of the snooty and distant people who work in them ever appears to exhibit any interest in their guests beyond enquiring after the expiry date of their company credit cards. And any town hosting thousands of television executives is bound to absorb into its fabric some of the cynicism and soullessness which colours the industry so deeply.

I often thought about the Borders while walking along the seafront at Cannes, going from one business meeting to another, while not listening to a bore at a cocktail party, or just looking out to sea beyond the hype and the chatter. And I thought about my family, once managing a long conversation with Bina between my hotel and the Palais. She was unimpressed. I doubt if much of it would have interested her either. As she got older the core of things mattered much more than show, or even disguise, and while the details of the deals I was involved in would have puzzled her, the substance, who was gaining an advantage over whom, would have been clear enough. It occurred to me that travel of this sort was slowly narrowing my mind, distancing me further and further from the sorts of lessons I wanted to learn, making me repeat myself often, taking up a great deal of time, building a core of boredom inside, corroding my energy.

But Bina would have understood the money all right. And in television I made some, and that sum did ultimately change how I lived. When the ITV franchises were put up for auction in the early 1990s, I was Director of Programmes at Scottish Television and centrally concerned with the business of regaining the right to broadcast for the next ten years and beyond. We won the game and each of the bid team was awarded a substantial bonus. I used mine to buy a ticket home.

After months of fruitless searching my wife and I found not so much a house in the Borders, as a view. We came across an old ruined cottage for sale in an acre of ground at the end of a long and rough track. What persuaded us was not the house but the site, and the immense vistas out to the west and the south. In fact the front door and the windows faced east because the prevailing wind blew down from the western hills, and most of the other houses in the valley had turned their backs in the same way. Two up, two down and with some ruinous loose boxes attached to one gable end, the property was not particularly remarkable. At least I didn't think so at the time. But in its original state, the house turned out to be very like those farm cottages where my family subsisted for many generations. Clearly a place could be, and was, made of it. What was most attractive was something less tangible. Each time we came to look at the house, and brought family and friends with us, we were reluctant to leave, often delaying departure until late in the evening. There was a settled peace about the place, and a powerful sense that others had felt the same thing over many generations. Certainly the house was old (although not listed, allowing us a free hand with rebuilding), and when the old roof was removed, the adzed boughs supporting the original thatch were found. And under the foundations of the loose boxes lay the remains of a much earlier building, perhaps something medieval. One summer, hidden by the long grass and the willowherb, I found a little standing stone down by the burn in the corner of what was to become a garden. By buying this house and its land and coming back to the Borders to live in a place where many people had lived before me, I felt I was rejoining a long continuum, finding my way back home, all the way home.

The practicalities of rebuilding and extending the old house descended into the familiar horrors of over-runs in time, money and materials, and after a year of forcing an unpleasant builder to do what he had contracted to do, we moved in in May 1994. My sister, Marjie, and her partner, Andy, gave us a May Tree, and a substantial consolation was that he had used all his architect's skills to design the rebuilt and extended house and one of my Hawick cousins, David, had done much of the beautiful masonry work.

At first we used the house for weekends, Christmas, Easter and summer holidays. It was a good way to conduct a delicate test. I spent all of my money (and much, much more) on the project because I wanted to have a reason to be in the Borders and already knew something of the tone and pace of life in a semi-rural community, but my wife had raised our children in the city. And they were emphatically city kids attending an urban primary school. Perhaps they would grow to dislike the country-side, miss the excitements and possibilities of the bright lights. Perhaps my wife would feel isolated, find the winter too difficult, the problems of communication too limiting. In the event the gradual and episodic nature of my family's introduction to the Borders seems to have persuaded them not only to accept but to actively enjoy life away from the city.

In late 1998 I realised that I had had enough of working in television management, and with the kindness and understand-ing of my colleagues at what had become Scottish Media Group, I resigned my directorship a few months later to try to make a living as a writer, journalist and producer of television pro-grammes, but most of all so that I could live permanently in the Borders. In order to avoid disrupting my kids' education at a crucial time I decided not to ask everyone to move with me, and to stay in the Borders house by myself during the week. I would have no distractions and no excuses.

It was a strange period. From working in large offices and TV studios with hundreds of other people, I began to work entirely on my own, sometimes talking to no-one for a day or two. From sitting through long days full of meetings and appointments, sud-denly I had to sort out my own routine, keep my own diary, do my own typing. From travelling to London at least once a week and further afield at least once a month, I had to commute from my bedroom to my office via the shower and the kitchen. The abruptness of these and other changes was mind-clearing, making me sort out what I wanted to do, the things that were most important to me. I had hankered after this life for a long time and in my mind had planned far ahead, but most of all I discovered that I wanted to be by myself for a time, to enjoy the quiet and the solitude.

Without consciously planning to do so, or really intending to spend much time or effort on it, I began thinking about my childhood in the Borders, and all of the unasked and unanswered questions about my Dad and where Bina came from. There is, I suppose, a point in anyone's life when they arrive at the blunt recognition that they have more past than future. But another, slightly different reason surfaced and pushed me to start asking questions, look at old birth certificates and wade through overgrown churchyards. I wanted to think about my childhood before it became too distant and before it acquired a rosy glow, and write not so much a memoir as an interim report. I am fifty-three and have, I hope, some time yet before the only appealing view is a backward one.

After more than four years of living in the Borders, I sometimes wonder why I ever left, and wasted so much time in aeroplanes. When the night sky is open and starlit, I can see the moving red and green lights of the London shuttle before the drone passes over my house. It is not that the Borders is a comfortable bolt-hole – it is not – or the life easy. Something much more intangible pinned me to this map. Perhaps I came back because history is a personal matter, and I feel myself part of it. Even though no member of my family has made a notable individual contribution, or achieved any great distinction, except playing rugby for Scotland, that is not the point, not the way to see it. What matters to me is that we were all Borderers who have been here for 400 years and likely much longer, who saw what happened here, helped make the landscape across which it all happened, and whose collective experience in one place made that place change.

Out of the window above the desk where I write this I can see the site of the Roman fort at Oakwood, the mound of the Norman fortress at Howden, a drove road snaking up the near horizon, the fields and hedges made by the agricultural improvers, and over by the stream that marks my southern boundary there is the shadow of a nineteenth-century tile works. Sitting on the step outside my office on a fine evening, I sometimes look at this landscape, and no matter how long ago they lived, prehistoric hunter-gatherers or eighteenth-century shepherds, I feel close to the nameless people who walked up this valley before I ever came to see it and to build a house on its northern slopes. In my mind the managed regiments of black-green spruces and sitkas on the far hillsides dissolve into the wild scrub and peat hags of the Ettrick Forest, the flat cultivated fields at the valley bottom carpet over with mossy hollows and willow copses, and the tarmacked B-road becomes a burnside track. When I found the small standing stone amongst the willowherb and nettles at the foot of what became a garden, it had collapsed almost flat and kicked out one side of its socket. But with a shovel and some fence posts, I managed to lever it upright again.

More than anyone it was Bina who brought me back here to this place, where I belong. If it had not been for her intervention, I should have left much earlier than I eventually did and without any doubt not felt the insistent tug of a homing instinct.

At Blanerne School, near Hawick, very few of the pupils saw the Borders as home. It was a boarding school where nothing was spared in the education of aristocratic children, not the rod or the cane, or any expense. From the mid-1950s my Dad worked there several times, rewiring the old mansion house where Mr Case ran his classes, with perhaps only thirty or so pupils whom he prepared for the Common Entrance examination. This allowed entry to Britain's public schools and clever children could win scholarships to the likes of Fettes, Glenalmond, even Eton and Harrow. Most came from wealthy, even aristocratic, families, and with his posse of teachers, Mr Case drilled them in irregular Latin verbs and mental arithmetic. After a year or two of going back and forth to Blanerne to do various jobs, my Dad became friendly with the headmaster and one Saturday morning he took me along to meet him. I had no idea that a purpose was afoot, we went to fix things at lots of big houses in the Borders. As soon as we arrived, Mr Case ushered us both into his study and invited me to sit down in a squeaky brown leather armchair. That was odd. We were usually down at the skirting board or up a ladder. And then he began to ask me questions about what I was interested in. Not much, I was only eight or nine. All I clearly remember of the conversation was that Mr Case's moustache waggled up and down when he spoke, and that he wore slippers outside, like Bina.

Back at No. 42 my Gran had made chips for Saturday dinner, and as I was munching mine, I watched my Dad go down the garden to talk to Ma. They talked for a long time, Ma looking at the ground a lot. I knew they were talking about me. And then my Dad and I went across to the rugby. It was Kelso against Hawick and some of my uncles and cousins were there. I don't recall the score, but I expect we lost, as usual. That night I remember exactly what went on. In return for something which was never made clear, perhaps work my Dad would do or had done, Mr Case was prepared to take me as a boarder at Blanerne School at no cost. I was still in the backward class making duff raffia mats at the time, so what was there to lose? Perhaps Ma had been convinced by that argument. After three years at Blanerne I would sit the Common Entrance and win a scholarship to a posh public school. And then get a good job with the other toffs. That was the plan. My Dad was keen, explaining how they had everything at these schools, everything anyone could want, swimming pools, that sort of thing, and Ma nodded her acquiescence. As they looked at me, all I could think was that they didn't want me any more, my Dad wanted rid of me. 'Stupid, just stupid. And cheeky to the teachers.' It was just like Dr Barnardo's or the Borstal, although I would be allowed out to come home at the weekends, sometimes, maybe. Didn't really know about that. Depended on the teachers. I just looked back at them, mouth no doubt wide open. And then after a time, from her chair over by the window, I heard Bina beginning to speak. Tears were streaming down her face. 'No. It's just not right,' she whispered, 'My wee lamb's not to go away from me. That's just not to happen.'

And it was enough. My Dad's resolve snapped immediately, the moment his mother spoke. 'Well, maybe not just now,' he said, meaning never, looking at my Ma. She sighed, shook her head and went back into the kitchen. I can see that he genuinely believed it to be a great chance for me, a radical departure that would have catapulted me into a different culture, far away from 42 Inchmead Drive, far from the farm places and the old ploughmen. It would be the making of me, set someone from nowhere on the road to somewhere. But in her old soul Bina knew that it was wrong, and when she spoke, her certainty needed only to be stated to have its power and touch my Ma and especially my Dad. All of the ancient bonds would have sundered. When I came back from these grand schools and alien places, if I came back, I would be different, sound different, no longer be the grandson of Bina, a child of the old life. After all that the power of blood and family had done to sustain her and my Dad's lives, Bina could not bear the thought of that loss. She would not see the bonds broken, not by a boy who would leave, leave it all behind, and would bear a name that meant little to him and less to any children who would bear it after. Bina would not have it, and she used all her power to save me. And to bring me home again.